"追求卓越"学英语丛书（英汉对照）

心灵的私语
——名人书信精选
Whisper of Soul: Letters from Famous People

◎ 主　编　谢艳明
◎ 副主编　年慧敏　赵　玲

河南大学出版社
HENAN UNIVERSITY PRESS

图书在版编目（CIP）数据

心灵的私语：名人书信精选：英汉对照／谢艳明主编.
开封：河南大学出版社，2008.4(2013.4重印)
("追求卓越"学英语丛书)
ISBN 978－7－81091－791－9

Ⅰ.心… Ⅱ.谢… Ⅲ.①英语—汉语—对照读物②书信集—世界 Ⅳ.H319.4：Ⅰ

中国版本图书馆CIP数据核字（2008）第035477号

责任编辑 程若春
封面设计 今日文教

出版发行	河南大学出版社			
	地址：河南省开封市明伦街85号		邮编：475001	
	电话：0378－2825001（营销部）		网址：www.hupress.com	
排　版	河南第一新华印刷厂			
印　刷	郑州市今日文教印制有限公司			
版　次	2008年4月第1版	印　次	2013年4月第2次印刷	
开　本	787mm×1092mm　1/16	印　张	12	
字　数	203千字	印　数	2001—3500册	
定　价	20.00元			

（本书如有印装质量问题请与河南大学出版社营销部联系调换）

前　言

"欲寄彩笺兼尺素,山长水阔知何处。"自古以来,书信就是人们工作、生活中主要的交往工具。从"尺素如残雪,结成双鲤鱼"到"烽火连三月,家书抵万金",书信曾经带给人们多少幸福、多少快乐啊！虽然等信的日子是那么让人难熬,可收到远方的祝福又该是多么让人欣喜若狂！

——家书,饱含着的自然是人间的亲情,在本书中我们可以读到马克·吐温的家书,读到的是亲情的自然流露,虽然家书中没有激情昂扬的言辞,但他那些对日常琐细的叙述,了却了家人的牵挂,宽慰了家人的心。

——情书,浸润着的却是恋人之间的美好爱情,法国女演员朱丽艾特·德萝艾特(Juliette Deroette)从1835年起就爱上了雨果,在此后的50年中,她给雨果写了许多热情洋溢的情书。尽管她的爱没有什么结果,但她的这份感情、这份执著却令人感动;即使骄傲的法兰西皇帝拿破仑对情人约瑟芬也是一封连一封地写情书,他可怜地呼唤道:"高贵的女士,你一天到晚在干些什么呢？什么事这么重要,竟使你没有时间给你忠诚的爱人写信？"我想:在这个时候,纵使已经发明了当代的移动电话,恐怕仍然难以抚慰这位皇帝大人的焦虑。"见字如见人",也许只有约瑟芬亲自给他写封信,才有可能让他如获至宝,心花怒放。

——本书还收录了朋友、同事之间的来信,不少还成了传世名作:如《海伦·凯勒致老师的书信》,此信中透露出海伦·凯勒和她老师之间深厚的友谊,那种师生感情是无法比拟的。

然而,源远流长几千年的写信传统,却在近年来渐行渐远,慢慢地走出了人们的视线。取而代之的是铺天盖地的移动短信,纵横驰骋的网络邮件,超越距离的视频聊天,特别是年轻人已经淡薄了手写信的概念,甚至号称现在已经进入了无纸化时代。

如今,也许只有三十多岁以上的朋友,才或多或少地还残存着一些关于手写信的记忆。那些记忆的呈现,既表明了世事的变迁,也在他们的心里留下了些许遗憾。难道不是吗？虽说现代通讯方式多样,信息传达迅速快捷,但早已形成了"言"而无"信"的尴尬局面:人们可以收到亲友的短信问候,但丧失了抚摸带着写信人体温信笺的感觉;能最快地听到亲友的声音,但丧失了咀嚼书信时的那种温馨和浪漫;可以在网上长篇大论,但丧失了将书信

串联起来、放在箱底珍藏时的那份执著与长久。

　　回顾过去,从过去的"言"而有"信",到如今的"言"而无"信",人们既感慨科技的进步,时代的发展,交流愈来愈方便快捷的喜人现实;可是另一方面,人们又不得不承认,人与人之间的心灵隔阂却不知为何也随之不断地加大了。拉近了遥远的声音,得到了快速的信息,却模糊了彼此的真实面目,触摸到的只是一张千篇一律的冰冷的面孔。这就是手写信与现代通讯的本质区别。

　　子在川上曰:"逝者如斯夫。"随着时间的流逝,我们可以看到:手机、电脑将马不停蹄地更新换代,曾经绚丽的"屏幕语言"将在时光的飞奔中消失殆尽,然而穿越时空的书信却越来越凸显优势,显得弥足珍贵。当一个白发苍苍的老人翻开往日的书信,他的心里将掀起怎样的巨涛狂澜?往事如烟,而亲人、朋友或是情人的书信,又让他回到了过去的年龄,慰藉着他寂寞、孤单的晚年。毫无疑问,书信是写信者文学才能、书法特性和礼仪品质的集中体现。所以阅读一封书信,就是在品读一个人,就是在体会一种人生。哦!你看那一封封泛黄的旧书信,定格着一段历史,流淌着一种体验,述说着一个故事。抱着一捆捆书信,我们将情不自禁地感叹:有书信的人生,才是一种别样的人生啊!

　　让我们静下心来重温读信的时代,在书信中穿越时空去仔细品味那种似曾相识的细腻情感,感受那份曾经的热情吧!

　　本书由赵玲负责编译第 1~34 篇、第 55 篇和附录部分,年慧敏负责编译第 35~54 篇。谢艳明负责全书的编写工作。由于编者的水平有限,书中错误在所难免,敬请各界读者不吝指正!

编者
2008 年 1 月

目 录

1. Henry Ⅷ's Love Letter to Anne Burline ……………………（1）
   亨利八世致安妮·博林的情书 ……………………………（2）
2. Henry Ⅳ's Love Letter to Gabrielle ………………………（3）
   亨利四世致加布里埃尔的情书 ……………………………（4）
3. Richard Steele's Love Letter to Mary Scurlock …………（5）
   理查德·斯梯尔致玛丽·斯卡洛克的情书 ………………（6）
4. Voltaire's Love Letter to Olympe Denover ………………（7）
   伏尔泰致奥琳普·邓诺弗的情书 …………………………（8）
5. Goethe's Love Letter to Charlotte von Stein ……………（9）
   歌德致夏洛特·冯·斯坦的情书 …………………………（10）
6. Mozart's Love Letter to Constanz …………………………（12）
   莫扎特致康斯坦兹的情书 …………………………………（13）
7. Robert Burns' Love Letter to an Unknown Lover ………（14）
   罗伯特·彭斯致神秘恋人的情书 …………………………（15）
8. Mary Wollstonecraft's Love Letter to William Godwin …（16）
   玛丽·沃斯通克拉夫特致威廉·戈德温的情书 …………（17）
9. Napoleon's Love Letters to Josephine ……………………（18）
   拿破仑致约瑟芬的情书 ……………………………………（20）
      其一 ……………………………………………………（20）
      其二 ……………………………………………………（20）
10. Beethoven's Love Letter ……………………………………（21）
    贝多芬的情书 ………………………………………………（22）
11. John Keats' Love Letters to Fanny Brawne ………………（23）
    约翰·济慈致范妮·布劳恩的情书 ………………………（24）
       其一 …………………………………………………（24）
       其二 …………………………………………………（25）
12. Victor Hugo's Love Letters to Adele Foucher ……………（26）
    维克托·雨果致阿黛尔·弗希尔的情书 …………………（28）
       其一 …………………………………………………（28）
       其二 …………………………………………………（29）

13. Juliette Deroette's Love Letter to Hugo ……………… (30)
    朱丽艾特·德萝艾特致雨果的情书 ………………………… (31)
14. Balzac's Love Letter to Evelina Hanska ……………… (32)
    巴尔扎克致艾弗琳娜·汉斯卡的情书 ……………………… (33)
15. Franz Liszt's Love Letters to Marie D'Agoult ……… (34)
    弗朗兹·李斯特致玛丽·达高特的情书 …………………… (36)
        其一 ……………………………………………………… (36)
        其二 ……………………………………………………… (37)
16. Robert Schumann's Love Letter to Clara Wieck …… (38)
    罗伯特·舒曼致克拉拉·维克的情书 ……………………… (39)
17. Stowe's Love Letter to Her Husband ………………… (41)
    斯托致丈夫的情书 ………………………………………… (43)
18. Flaubert's Love Letter to Louise Colet ……………… (45)
    福楼拜致路易莎·古内的情书 …………………………… (46)
19. Mark Twain's Love Letter to Olivia Langdon ……… (47)
    马克·吐温致奥利维亚·兰敦的情书 ……………………… (47)
20. Mark Twain's Letters to Mrs. Jane Clemens and Family …… (48)
    马克·吐温致夫人及家人 ………………………………… (53)
        其一 ……………………………………………………… (53)
        其二 ……………………………………………………… (54)
21. Mark Twain's Letter to Orion Clemens ……………… (56)
    马克·吐温致奥里恩·克莱门斯 …………………………… (59)
22. Lincoln's Letter to Horace Greeley …………………… (61)
    林肯致贺拉斯·格利里 …………………………………… (62)
23. Lincoln's Letter to George Robertson ……………… (64)
    林肯致乔治·罗伯逊 ……………………………………… (66)
24. Sullivan Ballou's Love Letter to His Wife …………… (67)
    萨利文·巴罗致妻子的情书 ……………………………… (70)
25. Lewis Carroll's Love Letter to Gertrude …………… (72)
    刘易斯·卡洛尔致格特鲁德的情书 ………………………… (73)
26. Robert Stevenson's Letter to Henry James ………… (75)
    罗伯特·斯蒂文森致亨利·詹姆斯 ………………………… (78)
27. Pierre Curie's Love Letter to Mary …………………… (80)

皮埃尔·居里致玛丽的情书 ……………………………… (81)
28. Jack London's Love Letter to Anna Strunsky ……………… (83)
　　杰克·伦敦致安娜·斯特伦斯基的情书 ………………… (84)
29. James Joyce's Love Letter to Nora Barnacle ……………… (86)
　　詹姆斯·乔伊斯致诺拉·巴纳克尔的情书 ……………… (87)
30. Rupert Brooke's Love Letter to Noel ……………………… (88)
　　鲁佩特·布鲁克致诺埃尔的情书 ………………………… (88)
31. Kafka's Love Letter to Felice ……………………………… (89)
　　卡夫卡致菲莉斯的情书 …………………………………… (90)
32. Bernard Shaw's Love Letter to Beatrice Campbell ………… (92)
　　萧伯纳致比阿特丽斯·坎贝尔的情书 …………………… (93)
33. Woodrow Wilson's Love Letter to Edith Galt ……………… (94)
　　伍德罗·威尔逊致伊迪丝·高尔特的情书 ……………… (95)
34. Katherine Mansfield's Love Letter to John Murry ………… (96)
　　凯瑟琳·曼斯菲尔德致约翰·穆里的情书 ……………… (97)
35. Helen Keller's Letters to Her Teacher ……………………… (99)
　　海伦·凯勒致老师 ………………………………………… (105)
　　　其一 …………………………………………………… (105)
　　　其二 …………………………………………………… (106)
36. Eleanor Roosevelt's Letter to Helen Keller ………………… (109)
　　艾琳娜·罗斯福致海伦·凯勒 …………………………… (110)
37. Helen Keller's Letter to Eleanor Roosevelt ………………… (111)
　　海伦·凯勒致艾琳娜·罗斯福 …………………………… (112)
38. Duff Cooper's Love Letter to Diana ……………………… (113)
　　达夫·库珀致黛安娜的情书 ……………………………… (114)
39. Zelda Sayre's Love Letter to Fitzgerald …………………… (115)
　　泽尔达·塞尔致菲茨杰拉德的情书 ……………………… (116)
40. Winston Churchill's Love Letter to Clemmie ……………… (117)
　　温斯顿·丘吉尔致克莱米的情书 ………………………… (118)
41. Winston Churchill's Letter to Franklin Roosevelt ………… (119)
　　温斯顿·丘吉尔致富兰克林·罗斯福 …………………… (121)
42. Franklin Roosevelt's Letter to Winston Churchill ………… (122)
　　富兰克林·罗斯福致温斯顿·丘吉尔 …………………… (123)

43. Franklin Roosevelt's Letter to Adolf Hitler ·················（124）
　　富兰克林·罗斯福致阿道夫·希特勒 ·····················（128）
44. Franklin D. Roosevelt's Letter to the American Federation of
　　Labor Convention ···（131）
　　富兰克林·D·罗斯福致美国劳工联盟大会 ···············（134）
45. Harry Truman's Letter to Kupcinet ·······················（136）
　　哈里·杜鲁门致库普辛那 ···（137）
46. President Kennedy's Letter to Governor Vandiver ····（138）
　　肯尼迪总统致范迪佛州长 ··（139）
47. Ronald Reagan's Love Letter to Nancy ···················（140）
　　罗纳德·里根致南希的情书 ······································（141）
48. Ronald Reagan's Letter to the American People ······（142）
　　罗纳德·里根致美国人民 ···（143）
49. Tom Watson's Letter of Resignation ·······················（145）
　　汤姆·华森的辞职信 ···（146）
50. Tony Blair's Letter to Tom Watson ·······················（148）
　　托尼·布莱尔致汤姆·华森 ····································（149）
51. Tony Blair's Letter to MFAW ································（150）
　　托尼·布莱尔致"反战军属" ··································（151）
52. MFAW's Letter to Tony Blair ································（153）
　　"反战军属"致托尼·布莱尔 ··································（155）
53. George W. Bush's Letter to Ariel Sharon ···············（157）
　　乔治·W.布什致阿里尔·沙龙 ·······························（161）
54. Ariel Sharon's Letter to George W. Bush ···············（164）
　　阿里尔·沙龙致乔治·W.布什 ·······························（168）
55. Model Love Letters 情书范文 ································（170）
　　Ⅰ. This Is My Love 这就是我的爱 ·······················（170）
　　Ⅱ. I'm Forever Yours 我永远属于你 ····················（171）
　　Ⅲ. You Are Special 你与众不同 ·····························（172）
　　Ⅳ. Tender Love 温柔的爱 ·····································（173）
　　Ⅴ. Forever 永远 ···（174）
附录：英文书信的组成 ···（180）

心灵的私语

Whisper of Soul: Letters from Famous People

1. Henry Ⅷ's Love Letter to Anne Burline

英国国王亨利八世(Henry Ⅷ,1491~1547)改变了16世纪欧洲的政治和宗教面貌,在决定与第一位妻子阿拉贡的凯瑟琳(Katherine of Aragon)离婚之后,他废除了天主教,建立了自己的英国国教。1533年,他与安妮·博林(Anne Burline)结婚,在下列信中他对安妮表达的爱却没有持续多久,安妮于1536年因其不贞而被处以极刑。

My mistress and my friend,

My heart and I surrender themselves into your hands, and we supplicate① to be commended② to your good graces, and that by absence your affection may not be diminished to us, for that would be to augment③ our pain, which would be a great pity, since absence gives enough, and more than I ever thought could be felt.

This brings to my mind a fact in astronomy, which is, that the further the poles are from the sun, notwithstanding④, the more searing is the heat. Thus it is with our love: absence has placed distance between us, nevertheless, fervor increases, at least on my part. I hope the same from you, assuring you that in my case the anguish⑤ of absence is so great that it would be intolerable⑥, were it not for the firm hope I have of your indissoluble⑦ affection towards me. In order to remind you of it, I send you the thing that comes nearest that is possible—that is to say, my picture set in bracelets, wishing myself in its place when it pleases you.

This is the hand of your servant and friend.

H. R.

① supplicate ['sʌplikeit] v. 恳求,请求
② commend [kə'mend] v. 称赞,表扬,推荐,委托
③ augment [ɔː'gment] v. 扩大,增加
④ notwithstanding [ˌnɔtwiθ'stændiŋ] conj. 虽然,尽管
⑤ anguish ['æŋgwiʃ] n. 剧痛,极度痛苦
⑥ intolerable [in'tɔlərəbl] adj. 无法忍受的,难耐的
⑦ indissoluble [ˌindi'sɔljubl] adj. 不能溶解的,不能分解的

亨利八世致安妮·博林的情书

我的情人,我的朋友:

我的身心都被你征服,听凭你的摆布,我们恳求得到你的宠爱。你的冷淡虽然打消不了我们对你的深情一片,却会增加我们的痛苦,这会多么令人遗憾,只因你的冷淡,我却苦不堪言。

这使我想到天文学中的一个事实:两极距离太阳越远,热量灼烧得却越厉害。如同你我之间的爱:你的冷淡让距离横亘在你我之间,然而,热情却增加了,至少在我这边。我希望你也会有和我一样的感受,你要知道,对我而言,若不是坚信你对我怀有不变的情感,你的冷淡给予我的伤害会让我无法忍耐。为了让你知道我对你的情感,我尽可能送你符合你心意的东西——也就是那个镶嵌在手镯里的画像,如果它使你快乐,我希望我能在它的位置上。

出自你忠诚的仆人和朋友之手。

亨利

2. Henry Ⅳ's Love Letter to Gabrielle

法国国王亨利四世(Henry Ⅳ,1553~1610)是波旁王朝的首任君主,他在政治上是一个娴熟的谈判家,在战场上是一个出色的士兵。下面的情书就是他在战场上写给加布里埃尔(Gabrielle)的。

June 16,1593

Dear Gabrielle,

    I have waited patiently for one whole day without news of you; I have been counting the time and that's what it must be. But a second day—I can see no reason for it, unless my servants have grown lazy or been captured by the enemy, for I dare not put the blame on you, my beautiful angel; I am too confident of your affection—which is certainly due to me, for my love was never greater, nor my desire more urgent①; that is why I repeat this refrain② in all my letters: come, come, come, my dear love. Honor with your presence the man who, if only he were free, would go a thousand miles to throw himself at your feet and never move from there.

    As for what is happening here, we have drained the water from the moat③, but our cannons④ are not going to be in place until Friday when I will dine in town.

    The day after you reach Mantes, my sister will arrive at Anet, where I will have the pleasure of seeing you every day. I am sending you a bouquet⑤ of orange blossom that I have just received. I kiss the hands of the Viscountess⑥ if she is there, and of my good friend, and as for you, my dear love, I kiss your feet a million times.

                                                         Henry

① urgent ['ɔːdʒənt] *adj.* 急迫的,紧急的
② refrain [ri'frein] *n.* 重复,叠句
③ moat [məut] *n.* 护城河,城壕
④ cannon ['kænən] *n.* 大炮,加农炮
⑤ bouquet ['bu(ː)kei, bu'kei] *n.* 花束
⑥ Viscountess ['vaikauntis] *n.* 子爵夫人,女子爵,指加布里埃尔的姐姐

亨利四世致加布里埃尔的情书

亲爱的加布里埃尔：

我耐心地等待，整整一天都没有你的消息。我一直在计算着时间，那是我必须做的事情。可是，第二天，我找不出任何理由收不到你的消息，除非我的仆人变懒或者被敌人俘去，只因我不敢责怪你，我美丽的安琪儿。我相信你对我的爱——它定会因我而存在，因为我从未感受过如此强烈的爱，如此热切的欲望。这就是我为什么在信中反复强调：亲爱的，来吧，来吧，来吧！你的出现会让一个人倍感荣幸，如果他是自由之身，他会走过迢迢千里跪倒在你的脚边，从此寸步不离。

至于这儿发生的事情，我们已经将战壕里的水抽干，但是我们的大炮直到星期五才能安装到位，那时，我才会进城用餐。

你抵达曼特斯之后，我的妹妹将到达阿内特，在那里我将会荣幸地每天都会和你见面。寄给你一束我刚刚收到的橙花。让我亲吻子爵夫人（如果她在那儿的话）和我的好朋友的手，至于你，亲爱的，我要无数次地亲吻你的脚。

亨利
1593 年 6 月 16 日

3. Richard Steele's Love Letter to Mary Scurlock

理查德·斯梯尔(Richard Steele, 1672~1729), 英国散文家和剧作家, 与约瑟夫·艾迪生(Joseph Addison)共同创办并编辑了《闲谈者》(1709~1711年)和《旁观者》(1711~1712年)。下面的情书是他在1707年写给玛丽·斯卡洛克(Mary Scurlock)的, 此情书写了不久, 他们就结婚了。他在一生中写了四百多封充满激情和智慧的情书。他死后, 玛丽·斯卡洛克将情书出售给出版商, 并获得很大一笔财富。

Madam,

I lay down last night with your image in my thoughts, and have awaked this morning in the same contemplation①. The pleasing transport with which I'm delighted, has a sweetness in it attended with a train of ten thousand soft desires, anxieties, and cares.

The day arises on my hopes with new brightness; youth beauty and innocence are the charming objects that steal me from myself, and give me joys above the reach of ambition②, pride or glory. Believe me, Fair One, to throw myself at your feet is giving myself the highest bliss③ I know of earth.

Oh hasten you minutes! Come over to me with happiness, and you will make me look down on Thrones④!

Richard Steele

---

① contemplation [ˌkɔntem'pleiʃən] n. 沉思; 凝视
② ambition [æm'biʃən] n. 野心, 雄心
③ bliss [blis] n. 福佑, 天赐的福
④ throne [θrəun] n. 王座, 君主

理查德·斯梯尔致玛丽·斯卡洛克的情书

夫人：

  昨晚，我躺在床上，脑海里全是你的影子；今天早晨醒来，我又这样想你。令我欣喜的马车载着甜蜜，里面还有无数温柔的期待、牵挂和关怀。

  在我的期待中迎来清新明亮的白昼。青春靓丽、清纯可爱的你如此迷人，让我魂不守舍。你给予我的快乐让抱负、骄傲和荣耀鞭长莫及。相信我，美丽的你，拜倒在你的脚下就是给了我天大的福气。

  加快你的步伐，快乐地来到我身边，你使得我对王位都不屑一顾！

理查德·斯梯尔

4. Voltaire's Love Letter to Olympe Denover

伏尔泰（Voltaire,1694~1778），法国作家和哲学家。19岁时，他就作为外交随从被派往荷兰。在那里，他爱上了贫民出身的奥琳普·邓诺弗（Olympe Denover）。他们的恋爱关系没有得到大使以及奥琳普的母亲的同意。为了将他们分开，大使将伏尔泰关进监狱。但不久，伏尔泰翻窗越狱，逃了出来。下面的情书就是伏尔泰在监狱里写给他的心上人的。

The Hague 1713

Dear Olympe,

  I am a prisoner here in the name of the King; they can take my life, but not the love that I feel for you. Yes, my adorable① mistress, to-night I shall see you, and I had to put my head on the block② to do it.

  For heaven's sake③, do not speak to me in such disastrous terms as you write; you must live and be cautious; beware of your mother as of your worst enemy. What do I say? Beware of everybody; trust no one; keep yourself in readiness, as soon as the moon is visible; I shall leave the hotel incognito④, take a carriage or a chaise⑤, we shall drive like the wind to Sheveningen; I shall take paper and ink with me; we shall write our letters.

  If you love me, reassure yourself, and call all your strength and presence of mind to your aid; do not let your mother notice anything, try to have your pictures, and be assured that the menace⑥ of the greatest tortures will not prevent me from serving you. No, nothing has the power to part me from you; our love is based upon virtue, and will last as long

---

① adorable [əˈdɔːrəbl] adj. 可爱的，迷人的
② block [blɔk] n. 断头台
③ for heaven's sake; for the benefit of heaven　看在上天的分上
④ incognito [inˈkɔgnitəu] adv. 隐姓埋名地
⑤ chaise [ʃeiz] n. 一种轻型马车
⑥ menace [ˈmenəs] n. 可能发生之危险；威胁

· 7 ·

as our lives. Adieu①, there is nothing that I will not brave for your sake; you deserve much more than that. Adieu, my dear heart!

Arout Voltaire

伏尔泰致奥琳普·邓诺弗的情书

亲爱的奥琳普：

  在这里，我是国王名义下的囚徒，他们能够夺走我的生命，却夺不走我对你的爱。是呵，我迷人的情人，今晚我要见到你，为此，我必须将自己的头放在断头台上。

  看在老天的分上，你写信的时候，不要对我说那些悲伤的话语。你必须活下去，要小心谨慎，小心你的母亲，她是你最大的敌人。我说什么呢？小心每一个人，谁都不要相信。月亮一露面，你就做好准备。我将离开这个未知的旅馆，乘上四轮马车或轻型马车，然后，我们会像风一样驾车到舍文宁根。我会带上纸和墨水，我们在那里写信。

  如果你爱我，你就尽管放心，使出你全身的力量，镇定自若，不要让你的母亲注意到什么，尽量带上你的图画，你要相信最大折磨的威胁也不能阻挡我来为你服务。不，什么都无法让你我分开。我们的爱是建立在美德之上的，并将一直延续到生命的结束。再见，为了你，我已无所畏惧，你也值得我为你付出。再见，我心爱的人！

阿劳特·伏尔泰
1713 年于海牙

---

① adieu [əˈdjuː] n. 再见

5. Goethe's Love Letter to Charlotte von Stein

约翰·沃尔夫冈·冯·歌德（Johann Wolfgang von Goethe, 1749~1832），德国著名作家和科学家，精通诗歌、歌剧和小说。他花了50年时间写了两部戏剧长诗《浮士德》。他还致力于各个领域的科学研究，在植物学方面享有盛誉，并在政府担任职务。下面的情书是他写给夏洛特·冯·斯坦（Charlotte von Stein）的。

June 17, 1784

Dear Charlotte,

My letters will have shown you how lovely I am.

I don't dine at Court, I see few people, and take my walks alone, and at every beautiful spot I wish you were there.

I can't help loving you more than is good for me; I shall feel all the happier when I see you again.

I am always conscious① of my nearness to you; your presence never leaves me.

In you I have a measure for every woman, for everyone; in your love a measure for all that is to be. Not in the sense that the rest of the world seems obscure, on the contrary, your love makes it clear; I see quite clearly what men are like and what they plan, wish, do and enjoy; I don't grudge② them what they have, and comparing is a secret joy to me, possessing as I do such an imperishable③ treasure. We often

---

① conscious [ˈkɔnʃəs] adj. 有意识的，有知觉的
② grudge [grʌdʒ] v. 吝惜，不愿意给或承认
③ imperishable [imˈperiʃəbl] adj. 不灭的，不朽的

don't notice objects simply because we don't choose to look at them, but things acquire an interest as soon as we see clearly the way they are related to each other.

The elephant's skull is coming with me to Weimar①.

My rock studies are going very well.

Fritz is happy and good. Without noticing it, he is taken into the world, and so without knowing it, he will become familiar with it. It is still all a game to him; yesterday I got him to read some petitions② and give me summaries of them; he laughed and wouldn't believe that people could be in such straits as these petitions made out.

Adieu, you whom I love a thousand times.

Johann

歌德致夏洛特·冯·斯坦的情书

亲爱的夏洛特:

我的信会向你展示我有多么可爱。

我不在宫廷里用餐,我很少与人相见,我独自散步,在每一个美丽的景点,我都希望你就在那儿。

我情不自禁地爱着你,超出了我爱自己,能够再见到你会让我幸福无比。

我总是有意识地接近你,我总是关注你的存在。

在你身上,我找着了对每一个女人,对每个人的衡量尺寸;在你的爱中,我也找着了对所有爱的测量标准。我并不是说,世界其他地方显得模糊不清,而刚好相反,你的爱使得那里清清楚楚。我很清

---

① Weimar [ˈvaimɑː] 魏玛,德国中部莱比锡西南的城市。在1775年歌德到达后,它逐渐发展成为德国最重要的文化中心。1919年,德国国民代表大会在此召开,建立了魏玛共和国,该共和国1933年灭亡。

② petition [piˈtiʃən] n. 请愿,请愿书,诉状

楚地看见人是什么样子，他们在计划什么，希望什么，做什么以及享受什么。我不妒忌他们的所有。攀比是我内心的乐趣，像我这样的拥有才是永恒的财富。我们常常看不见物体，只是因为我们不想去看它们，但是一旦我们看清了事物之间的联系方式，我们就会对它们发生兴趣。

我将带着大象的头盖骨到魏玛。

我的岩石研究进展很好。

弗里兹很快乐也很好。他还来不及注意就被带进这个世界，所以不需要刻意了解，他就熟悉了周围的世界。世界对他仍然是场游戏；昨天我要他阅读一些诉状，并要他概述。他笑了，不相信人民处在诉状所说的这种困境中。

再见，一千倍地爱你！

约翰
1784年6月17日

6. Mozart's Love Letter to Constanz

沃尔夫冈·阿马戴乌斯·莫扎特(Wolfgang Amadeus Mozart,1756~1791),奥地利作曲家,被认为是历史上最伟大、最有成就的作曲家之一。在他的600余篇作品中,最出色的作品,包括他最后三首交响乐(1788年)和歌剧《唐·乔万尼》(Don Giovanni,1787)和《魔笛》(The Magic Flute,1791),是在他短暂生命的最后五年里写成的。下面的情书是他写给妻子康斯坦兹(Constanz)的信的一部分。

Mainz①, October 17,1790

Dear Constanz,

While I was writing the last page, tear after tear fell on the paper. But I must cheer up—catch! —An astonishing number of kisses are flying about—The deuce! —I see a whole crowd of them! Ha! Ha! I have just caught three—They are delicious! —You can still answer this letter, but you must address your reply to Linz②. As I do not yet know for certain whether I shall go to Regensburg③, I can't tell you anything definite. Just write on the cover that the letter is to be kept until called for.

Adieu—Dearest, most beloved little wife—Take care of your health—and don't think of walking into town. Do write and tell me how you like our new quarters—Adieu. I kiss you millions of times.

Wolfgang

---

① Mainz [maints] 美因兹,德国中西部的一个城市,位于法兰克福西南偏西方向,莱茵河和美因河的交汇处。

② Linz [lints] 林茨,奥地利北部城市,位于维也纳西部多瑙河畔。

③ Regensburg ['reigənsbəːg] 雷根斯堡,德国东南部在多瑙河边上的一个城市,位于慕尼黑东北偏北方向。

莫扎特致康斯坦兹的情书

亲爱的康斯坦兹：

　　当我写到最后一页，眼泪不住地滴在纸上。但我必须振作起来——接住！——无数令人惊奇的吻飞来——打平了！——我看见香吻蜂拥而至！哈哈！我接住了三个——它们的味道甜蜜！你可以回这封信，但是你必须寄到林茨。因为我不能肯定地知道我是不是去雷根斯堡，所以不能确切地告诉你任何东西。就在封面上写，信要保存到我去取为止。

　　再见，亲爱的，我至爱的贤妻——多多保重身体——别想着进城。一定要写信给我，并告诉我你喜不喜欢我们的新居——再见。吻你一百万遍。

沃尔夫冈
1790 年 10 月 17 日于美因兹

7. Robert Burns' Love Letter to an Unknown Lover

罗伯特·彭斯(Robert Burns, 1759~1796),苏格兰诗人,代表作有:《我的心呀在高原》、《一朵红红的玫瑰》和《自由树》。彭斯用苏格兰方言写作,继承、发掘了民间歌谣的传统,把诗与歌紧紧结合起来,纯朴自然,极富乡土气息。

Dear Madam,

The passion of love has need to be productive of much delight; as where it takes thorough possession of the man, it almost unfits him for anything else.

The lover who is certain of an equal return of affection, is surely the happiest of men; but he who is a prey to the horrors of anxiety and dreaded disappointment, is a being whose situation is by no means enviable①.

Of this, my present experience gives me much proof.

To me, amusement seems impertinent②, and business intrusion③, while you alone engross④ every faculty of my mind.

May I request you to drop me a line, to inform me when I may wait upon you?

For pity's sake, do; and let me have it soon.

In the meantime allow me, in all the artless sincerity of truth, to assure you that I truly am, my dearest Madam.

Your ardent⑤ lover, and devoted humble servant

Robert Burns

---

① enviable ['enviəbl] *adj.* 令人羡慕的,可羡慕的
② impertinent [im'pə:tinənt] *adj.* 无关的,鲁莽的,不相干的
③ intrusion [in'tru:ʒən] *n.* 闯入,侵扰
④ engross [in'grəus] *v.* 吸引注意,占用时间,使全神贯注
⑤ ardent ['ɑ:dənt] *adj.* 热心的,热情洋溢的,激烈的

罗伯特·彭斯致神秘恋人的情书

亲爱的女士：

　　爱的激情有必要制造出许多乐趣。它需要完全地占有某个人,因而使得他不适合其他任何事情。

　　有把握得到同样感情回报的人肯定是最快乐的人,但是如果他被忧虑所困扰,被可怕的失望所吞噬,那他的境况绝不令人羡慕。

　　就这一点,我现在的经历给了我许多证据。

　　对我而言,娱乐似乎无关紧要,做事也是迫不得已,因为你一人占据了我的全部思维。

　　能不能请求你给我写封信,告诉我要等你多久?

　　求求你,写封信吧,让我尽快收到它。

　　同时请允许我用完全朴实的真诚向你保证我是认真的,我亲爱的女士。

　　你的热情的爱人,忠诚谦卑的仆人

罗伯特·彭斯

8. Mary Wollstonecraft's Love Letter to William Godwin

玛丽·沃斯通克拉夫特(Mary Wollstonecraft)是爱尔兰的女权运动者和作家。她与第一个丈夫吉尔伯特·因姆来结婚,生下女儿范妮,就被丈夫抛弃,为此,她跳进泰晤士河,差点被淹死。后来,她遇上了威廉·戈德温(William Godwin)。爱情使得他们于1797年3月29日走到了一起。然而,就在那一年,她死于难产。而她所生的玛丽长大后嫁给了著名诗人雪莱,并写下了《法兰肯斯坦》(Frankenstein)。

October 4, 1796

My Dear,

I would have liked to dine with you today, after finishing your essay, that my eyes, and lips, I do not exactly mean my voice, might have told you that they had raised you in my esteem. What a cold word! I would say love, if you will promise not to dispute about its propriety, when I want to express an increasing affection, founded on a more intimate① acquaintance with your heart and understanding.

I shall cork up all my kindness—yet the fine volatile② essence may fly off in my walk—you know not how much tenderness for you may escape in a voluptuous③ sigh, should the air, as is often the case, give a pleasurable movement to the sensations, that have been clustering round my heart, as I read this morning—reminding myself, every now and then, that the writer loved me.

Voluptuous is often expressive of a meaning I do not now intend to give, I would describe one of those moments, when the senses are exactly tuned by the ringing tenderness of the heart and according reason entices you to live in the present moment, regardless of the past or future—it is

---

① intimate [ˈintimit] adj. 亲密的,隐私的
② volatile [ˈvɔlətail] adj. 挥发性的,不稳定的
③ voluptuous [vəˈlʌptuəs] adj. 骄奢淫逸的

not rapture①—it is sublime② tranquility③.

I have felt it in your arms—hush! Let not the light see, I was going to say hear it—these confessions should only be uttered—you know where, when the curtains are up—and all the world shut out—Ah me!

I wish I may find you at home when I carry this letter to drop it in the box,—that I may drop a kiss with it into your heart, to be embalmed④, till we meet, closer.

Mary

玛丽·沃斯通克拉夫特致威廉·戈德温的情书

我的亲爱的:

  今天,你写完文章之后,我本想与你一同进餐的,我的眼睛和嘴唇(我并不是说我的声音)也许已告诉你我对你敬重有加。多么冷酷的词啊! 当我想用爱表达一种越来越浓的情感的时候,如果你保证不争论爱的方式,我想说爱是建立在对你的心更亲密的熟悉和理解之上的。

  我要用塞子将我的温柔塞住——我散步时,这一易挥发的精髓可能会飞走——你不知道如果空气像往常一样让感觉愉快地运动,在一声骄奢的叹息中,多少属于你的、积聚在我心头的温柔会逃走。今天早晨我阅读的时候,我不断地提醒自己那个写作的人爱着我。

  骄奢通常很好地表达我现在不想表达的意思,我想描述那一刻,感官被心中叮叮作响的温柔调得恰如其分,相应的理由诱惑着你生活在此刻,不管过去和将来——不是欢天喜地——而是庄严肃静。

  我已经在你的怀中感到了它——安静! 不要让光线看见,我要说听吧——这些坦白就该说出声——你知道何时何地窗帘大开——全世界都关闭了——哎哟!

  当我拿着这封信准备投进邮箱时,我希望能在家里看到你,我也寄上我的吻,送进你的心田,让你保存,直到我能更近地见到你。

玛丽
1796 年 10 月 4 日

---

① rapture [ˈræptʃə] n. 全神贯注,兴高采烈
② sublime [səˈblaim] adj. 崇高的,高尚的,令人崇敬的
③ tranquility [trænˈkwiliti] n. 平静,安静
④ embalm [imˈbɑːm] v. 铭记于心,使不朽

9. Napoleon's Love Letters to Josephine

　　拿破仑·波拿巴(Napoleon Bonaparte,1769~1821)出生于科西嘉岛,1785年,他成为一名军官。1799年,他发动政变,成为法国首席执政官。1804年,他当上法国皇帝。除了具有出色的军事才能和钢铁般的意志之外,他还是个多产的书信作家,尤其擅长写作柔情绵绵的情书。下面的两封情书是他写给美丽的妻子约瑟芬(Josephine)的。在1804年到1810年期间,他在欧洲扩疆拓土,建立了军事强大的帝国。1814年,他出征俄罗斯,遭遇失败,被迫放弃皇位。1815年,他重新夺得政权,在滑铁卢战役中遭到了决定性的失败,被流放到圣海伦娜岛,一直到1821年去世。

I

Paris, December 1795

Dear Josephine,

　　I wake filled with thoughts of you. Your portrait and the intoxicating① evening which we spent yesterday have left my senses in turmoil②. Sweet, incomparable Josephine, what a strange effect you have on my heart! Are you angry? Do I see you looking sad? Are you worried? My soul aches with sorrow, and there can be no rest for you; I yield to the profound feelings which overwhelm me and I draw from your lips, from your heart a love which consumes me with fire. Ah! it was last night that I fully realized how false an image of you your portrait gives!

　　You are leaving at noon; I shall see you in three hours.

　　Until then, a thousand kisses; but give me none in return, for they set my blood on fire.

Napoleon

---

① intoxicating [in'tɔksikeitiŋ] adj. 醉人的,使人兴奋的
② turmoil ['tə:mɔil] n. 骚动,混乱

II

Spring 1797

To Josephine,

　　I love you no longer; on the contrary, I detest you. You are a wretch, truly perverse①, truly stupid, a real Cinderella②. You never write to me at all, you do not love your husband; you know the pleasure that your letters give him yet you cannot even manage to write him half a dozen lines, dashed off in a moment! What then do you do all day, Madame? What business is so vital that it robs you of the time to write to your faithful lover? What attachment③ can be stifling④ and pushing aside the love, the tender and constant love which you promised him? Who can this wonderful  new lover be who takes up your every moment, rules your days and nights and prevents you from devoting your attention to your husband?

　　Beware, Josephine; one fine night the doors will be broken down and there I shall be. In truth, I am worried, my love, to have no news from you; write me a four-page letter instantly made up from those delightful words which fill my heart with emotion and joy. I hope to hold you in my arms before long, when I shall lavish⑤ upon you a million kisses, burning as the equatorial⑥ sun.

Napoleon

---

　　① perverse [pə(ː)ˈvəːs] adj. 反复无常的,不正当的,堕落的
　　② Cinderella [ˌsindəˈrelə] 灰姑娘,童话中的美丽姑娘,被后母虐待,终日与煤渣为伴,后来逃脱出来并嫁给了王子。
　　③ attachment [əˈtætʃmənt] n. 依恋,爱慕
　　④ stifle [ˈstaifl] v. 使窒息,抑制
　　⑤ lavish [ˈlæviʃ] v. 浪费,滥用,慷慨给予
　　⑥ equatorial [ˌekwəˈtɔːriəl] adj. 近赤道的,赤道的

拿破仑致约瑟芬的情书

其　一

亲爱的约瑟芬：

　　我无法入睡,头脑里全想着你。你的画像和昨晚我们一起度过的醉人时光让我的思维一片混乱。甜蜜的、无人比拟的约瑟芬,你对我的心产生了多么奇特的效应！你生气了吗？你悲伤吗？你焦虑吗？我的灵魂因为悲伤而感到疼痛,想到你,我的内心无法安宁,我屈服于将我淹没的深深的感情,我从你的嘴唇里、从你的心中抽出将我烧为灰烬的爱。啊！就在昨晚,我彻底认识到你的肖像画绘出的是一个多么错误的形象！

　　你中午就要出发,我三小时后与你相见。

　　到那时,给你无数个吻,但我不需要你任何回报,因为你的吻会让我的血液燃烧。

拿破仑
1795年12月于巴黎

其　二

致约瑟芬：

　　我不再爱你;恰好相反,我恨你。你是个倒霉的人,真的很反常,很愚蠢,一个真正的灰姑娘。你从不给我写信,你不爱你的丈夫。你知道你的信会给他带去多大的快乐！你连几行都写不了,就草草了事。那么,夫人,你整天在干什么？什么事那么重要,竟然抢去了你给你忠诚的爱人写信的时间？是什么样的恋情如此令人窒息,让你将爱,将你许诺的、温柔的、永恒的爱放在一边？谁会是这个神奇的第三者？他占有了你每个时刻,统治着你的白天和黑夜,阻止了你将关心献给你的夫君！

　　请你小心,约瑟芬！某个美妙的夜晚,我会破门而入。真的,我的爱,收不到你的任何消息我很担心,赶快给我写四页纸的信,措词要优美动听,使我的内心充满激情和欢欣。我希望不久就能拥你入怀,并非常慷慨地给你一百万个吻,像赤道的太阳一样灼灼烧人。

拿破仑
1797年春

10. Beethoven's Love Letter

路德维希·梵·贝多芬是历史上最著名最富有传奇色彩的作曲家。他在57岁去世的时候，留下了一个秘密：人们在他的遗物里发现了一封情书，是写给一位不知姓名的女人的，贝多芬只把她叫做"我永远的爱"。世人毫不知晓这位神秘女人，也不了解这场爱情的前因后果，只有信件表明他曾经有过一次刻骨铭心的爱情，和那些使他成名的乐曲一样热烈。《月光曲》还有其他许多协奏曲都隐隐表露出这个不为人知的爱情悲剧。

July 6, 1806

My angel, my all, my very self—only a few words today and at that with your pencil—not till tomorrow will my lodgings be definitely determined upon—what a useless waste of time. Why this deep sorrow where necessity speaks—can our love endure except through sacrifices—except through not demanding everything—can you change it that you are not wholly mine, I not wholly thine①?

Oh, God! Look out into the beauties of nature and comfort yourself with that which must be—love demands everything and that very justly—that it is with me so far as you are concerned, and you with  me. If we were wholly united you would feel the pain of it as little as I!

Now a quick change to things internal② from things external③. We shall surely see each other; moreover, I cannot communicate to you the observations I have made during the last few days touching my own life—

---

① thine [ðain] *pron.* 你的东西，你的
② internal [in'tə:nl] *adj.* 内在的
③ external [eks'tə:nl] *adj.* 外部的

if our hearts were always close together I would make none of the kind. My heart is full of many things to say to you—Ah!—there are moments when I feel that speech is nothing after all—cheer up—remain my true, only treasure, my all as I am yours; the gods must send us the rest that which shall be best for us.

Your faithful,
Ludwig

贝多芬的情书

  我的天使,我的所有,我的自我——今天虽然寥寥数语还是用你的铅笔所写——直到明天才能决定我的栖身之处——这多么浪费光阴啊!为什么必须道出这深深的哀愁——难道只有做出牺牲,一无所求,我们的爱情才能长久——你并非完全属于我,我也并非完全属于你,难道你能将这一事实改变?

  啊,上帝!留意一下自然之美,在其中找寻必要的安慰——爱情要求完美,这是理所当然——正如你所关心的那样,你要和我在一起,而且只有我和你。如果我们真正结合在一起,你就会像我一样感觉不到痛苦的存在!

  而今,情况由内到外变化极快。我们定会见到彼此;而且,我无法告诉你在最后这段影响我生命的日子里我所做的观察——如果我们的心永远紧紧相连在一起,对此我会只字不提。我心中有千言万语向你倾诉——啊!——可是,此刻语言是多么苍白无力——振作起来吧——做我唯一的真正宝贝,我的所有,因为我是你的;诸神必将给我们最好的礼物。

你忠诚的
路得维希
1806年7月6日

11. John Keats' Love Letters to Fanny Brawne

约翰·济慈(John Keats,1795~1821),英国最伟大的诗人之一,他的作品音调优美,古典意象丰富。他在短暂的一生中创作了不朽的名篇佳作。23 岁的时候,他爱上了邻居女孩范妮·布劳恩(Fanny Brawne)。不幸的是,那时医生已经诊断出他患上了最终导致他英年早逝的肺结核,所以,他们之间的爱情不可能走向美好的婚姻。以下是济慈写给范妮·布劳恩的两封热情洋溢的情书。

I

March 1820

Sweetest Fanny,

  You fear, sometimes, I do not love you so much as you wish? My dear Girl I love you ever and ever and without reserve. The more I have known you the more have I loved. My jealousies have been agonies① of Love, and in the hottest fit I would have died for you. I have vexed② you too much. But for Love! Can I help it? You are always new. The last of your kisses was ever the sweetest; the last smile the brightest; the last movement the gracefulest. When you passed my window home yesterday, I was filled with as much admiration as if I had then seen you for the first time.

  Have I nothing else then to love in you but that? Do not I see a heart naturally furnished with wings imprison itself with me? No ill prospect has been able to turn your thoughts a moment from me. This perhaps should be as much a subject of sorrow as joy—but I will not talk of that. Even if you did not love me I could not help an entire devotion to you: how much more deeply then must I feel for you knowing you love me. I

---

① agony ['ægəni] n. 极度痛苦
② vex [veks] v. 使痛苦,使受难

never felt my Mind repose upon anybody with complete and undistracted① enjoyment—upon no person but you. When you are in the room my thoughts never fly out of the window: you always concentrate my whole senses.

Your affectionate,

J. Keats

II

Sweetest Fanny,

I cannot exist without you—I am forgetful of everything but seeing you again—my life seems to stop there—I see no further. You have absorbed me.

I have a sensation at the present moment as though I were dissolving—I have been astonished that men could die martyrs② for religion—I have shuddered③ at it—I shudder no more—I could be martyred for my religion—love is my religion—I could die for that—I could die for you. My creed is love and you are its only tenet④—you have ravished⑤ me away by a power I cannot resist.

John Keats

约翰·济慈致范妮·布劳恩的情书

其 一

最亲爱的范妮：

你是不是有时担心我不像你希望的那样爱你？我亲爱的姑娘，我永远永远永远爱你，毫不保留。我越了解你就越爱你。我的嫉妒之心成了爱的

---

① undistracted [ˌʌndɪsˈtræktɪd] adj. 不分心的，注意力集中的
② martyr [ˈmɑːtə] n. 烈士，殉教者
③ shudder [ˈʃʌdə] v. 战栗，发抖
④ tenet [ˈtiːnet, ˈtenɪt] n. 教义，信条，原则
⑤ ravish [ˈrævɪʃ] v. 用武力抓住或夺取

痛苦,在最热烈的感情冲动中,我几乎为你而死。我对你如此恼怒,但是为了爱,有什么法子?你总是每天不同,你最后的吻最甜蜜;最后的微笑最靓丽;最后的动作最优美。你昨日回家时经过我的窗外,爱慕之情在我心中荡漾,宛若第一次见到你一样。

除了爱你,我还有什么?难道我没看见一颗天生翅膀的心随我一同被监禁?任何坏的期望也不能让我片刻不想你,这也许既是悲伤的主题,也是欢乐的主题,但我不愿谈起。即使你不爱我,我也禁不住对你全心投入:我该投入多深的感情才会让我知道你爱我。我从没有感到我的头脑会以完完全全、不受干扰的快乐为某个人停歇,除了你,再没有他人。当你待在我的房间里的时候,我的思绪从不飞出窗外:你总是使我的感官全神贯注。

你的挚爱

约翰·济慈

1820 年 3 月

其　二

最亲爱的范妮:

没有你,我无法生存,我容易忘记一切,但忘不了再次与你相见,我的生命似乎在那里停留,我看不见更远的地方,你将我全部吸收。

此刻,我有一种感觉,似乎正被溶解——人们为宗教而献身让我钦佩不已——我曾经为这种壮举感到战栗——而此刻却不再战栗——我也能为我的宗教献身——爱就是我的宗教——我可以为之牺牲——我可以为你而死。我的信条就是爱,而你是其唯一的教义——你用我无法抗拒的力量将我掠去。

约翰·济慈

12. Victor Hugo's Love Letters to Adele Foucher

维克托·雨果(Victor Hugo,1802~1885),法国作家,1851年拿破仑掌权后被驱逐,1870年返回法国。他的小说包括《巴黎圣母院》(1831)和《悲惨世界》(1862)。雨果从小就跟阿黛尔·弗希尔(Adele Foucher)一起长大,17岁时疯狂地爱上了她。虽然双方父母都表示反对,但他们仍然秘密地私订终身,并决意要结为夫妻。

I

Friday evening, March 15, 1822

Dear Adele,

After the two delightful evenings spent yesterday and the day before, I shall certainly not go out tonight, but will sit here at home and write to you. Besides, my Adele, my adorable① and adored Adele, what have I not to tell you? O, God! for two days, I have been asking myself every moment if such happiness is not a dream. It seems to me that what I feel is not of earth. I cannot yet comprehend this cloudless heaven.

You do not yet know, Adele, to what I had resigned myself. Alas, do I know it myself? Because I was weak, I fancied I was calm; because I was preparing myself for all the mad follies of despair, I thought I was courageous and resigned. Ah! Let me cast myself humbly at your feet, you who are so grand, so tender and strong! I had been thinking that the utmost limit of my devotion could only be the sacrifice② of my life; but you, my generous love, were ready to sacrifice for me the repose③ of yours.

---

① adorable [ə'dɔːrəbl] *adj.* 可崇拜的,可爱的
② sacrifice ['sækrifais] *n. & v.* 牺牲,献身
③ repose [ri'pəuz] *n.* 休息,睡眠,静止

You have been privileged to receive every gift from nature; you have both fortitude① and tears. Oh, Adele, do not mistake these words for blind enthusiasm②—enthusiasm for you has lasted all my life, and increased day by day. My whole soul is yours. If my entire existence had not been yours, the harmony of my being would have been lost, and I must have died—died inevitably.

These were my meditations③, Adele, when the letter that was to bring me hope or else despair arrived. If you love me, you know what must have been my joy.

My Adele, why is there no word for this but joy? Is it because there is no power in human speech to express such happiness?

The sudden bound from mournful④ resignation to infinite felicity⑤ seemed to upset me. Even now I am still beside myself and sometimes I tremble lest I should suddenly awaken from this dream divine⑥.

Oh, now you are mine! At last you are mine! Soon—in a few months, perhaps, my angel will sleep in my arms, will awaken in my arms, and will live there. All your thoughts at all moments, all your looks will be for me; all my thoughts, all my moments, all my looks will be for you! My Adele!

Adieu, my angel, my beloved Adele! Adieu! I will kiss your hair and go to bed. Still I am far from you, but I can dream of you. Soon perhaps you will be at my side. Adieu; pardon the delirium⑦ of your husband who embraces you, and who adores you, both for this life and another.

Yours forever,

Victor Hugo

---

① fortitude ['fɔːtitjuːd] n. 坚韧
② enthusiasm [in'θjuːziæzəm] n. 热情
③ meditation [medi'teiʃən] n. 沉思，冥想
④ mournful ['mɔːnful] adj. 悲哀的
⑤ felicity [fi'lisiti] n. 幸福，幸运，福气
⑥ divine [di'vain] adj. 神的，神圣的
⑦ delirium [di'liriəm] n. 精神错乱，发狂，极度兴奋

II

1821

My dearest,

When two souls, which have sought each other for, however long in the throng, have finally found each other... a union, fiery and pure, begins on earth and continues forever in heaven.

This union is love, true love, ... a religion, which deifies the loved one, whose life comes from devotion and passion, and for which the greatest sacrifices are the sweetest delights.

This is the love which you inspire in me... Your soul is made to love with the purity and passion of angels; but perhaps it can only love another angel, in which case I must tremble with apprehension.

Yours forever,

Victor Hugo

维克托·雨果致阿黛尔·弗希尔的情书

其 一

亲爱的阿黛尔：

度过了昨天和前天两个愉快夜晚之后，我今晚肯定不会出去，我要坐在家里，写信给你。另外，我的阿黛尔，我可爱的并珍爱的阿黛尔！我有什么没跟你讲？啊，上帝！两天来，我每时每刻都在问自己，这种幸福该不是梦吧？我的感觉似乎不是实实在在的，我无法理解这种晴空万里。

阿黛尔，你还不知道我将自己托付给了谁。哎呀，我自己知道吗？因为软弱，我想象自己很镇定；因为我在准备面对绝望的疯狂荒唐，我想象自己勇气十足并听天由命。啊！让我谦卑地拜倒在你的脚前，你是那样的伟大，那样的温柔，那样的无法抵御！我一直想我最大极限的奉献可能只会是牺牲自己的生命；而你，我慷慨的爱，准备为我献出你平静的生活。

你有特权去接受大自然给你的每一个礼物，你既有坚强的意志，也有软弱的眼泪。啊，阿黛尔，别将这些词语误解为盲目的热情，我对你的热情持续了我的一生，并且在与日俱增。我的整个灵魂都属于你。如果我整个的生存不是为了你,那我生命的和谐就会失去,那我早就死了——肯定早就死了。

这些就是我的沉思默想,阿黛尔,你要收到的这封信将给我带来希望或者绝望。如果你爱我,你就知道我的欢乐一直是什么。

我的阿黛尔,为什么只有"欢乐"一词才能说明这些?是否因为人类语言无力表达这一快乐?

从悲哀的放弃到无限的幸福这一突然飞跃似乎把我弄糊涂了。甚至到了现在,我还在彷徨恍惚,有时,我感到战栗,唯恐我突然从这一美妙的梦中醒来。

啊,现在你属于我了!你终于成了我的!很快——也许几个月后,我的天使就会在我的怀中入睡,在我的怀中醒来,并永远生活在我的怀中。你任何时刻的任何想法,你的任何样子都将为了我;我的所有想法,所有时刻,所有的样子也是为了你!我的阿黛尔!

再见,我的天使,我心爱的阿黛尔,再见!我将吻着你的头发上床睡觉,尽管我离你很遥远,但我能够梦见你。很快你就会躺在我身旁。再见,请原谅你丈夫的精神错乱,他无论今生还是来世都拥抱你,珍爱你。

永远是你的

维克托·雨果
1822 年 3 月 15 日,星期五晚

其 二

我最亲爱的:

当两个灵魂在人群中长久地相互寻觅,并终于找着了彼此时,一种火热而且纯净的结合就在人间开始,并且会在天堂永远继续。

这种结合就是爱,真实的爱……是一种宗教,将被爱的人神化,她的生命来自于忠诚和热情,为了她,最大的牺牲就是最大的快乐。

这就是你在我心中激起的爱……你的灵魂生来就是要带着天使的纯净和热情去爱;可能它只会去爱另外一个天使,这样一来,我肯定会忧虑地颤抖。

永远是你的

维克托·雨果
1821 年

13. Juliette Deroette's Love Letter to Hugo

法国女演员朱丽艾特·德萝艾特(Juliette Deroette)从1835年起就爱上了雨果,在此后的50年中,她给雨果写了许多热情洋溢的情书。

Friday 8 p.m.

Dear Victor,

If only I were a clever woman, I could describe to you my gorgeous① bird, how you unite in yourself the beauties of form, plumage②, and song!

I would tell you that you are the greatest marvel of all ages, and I should only be speaking the simple truth. But to put all this into suitable words, my superb one, I should require a voice far more harmonious③ than that which is bestowed upon④ my species—for I am the humble owl that you mocked at only lately, therefore, it cannot be.

I will not tell you to what degree you are dazzling and to the birds of sweet song who, as you know, are none the less beautiful and appreciative.

I am content to delegate to them the duty of watching, listening and admiring, while to myself I reserve the right of loving; this may be less attractive to the ear, but it is sweeter far to the heart.

I love you, I love you. My Victor; I can not reiterate⑤ it too often; I can never express it as much as I feel it.

I recognize you in all the beauty that surrounds me in form, in color, in perfume, in harmonious sound. You are superior to all. I see and admire—you are all!

You are not only the solar spectrum with the seven luminous⑥

---

① gorgeous ['gɔːdʒəs] adj. 耀眼的,美丽的,眩目艳丽的
② plumage ['pluːmidʒ] n. 全身羽毛
③ harmonious [hɑːˈməunjəs] adj. 和谐的,协调的
④ bestow upon 赠与,授予
⑤ reiterate [riːˈitəreit] v. 重申,重复说或者做
⑥ luminous ['ljuːminəs] adj. 发光的,明亮的

colors, but the sun himself, that illumines, warms, and revivifies①! This is what you are, and I am the lowly woman that adores you.

Juliette

朱丽艾特·德萝艾特致雨果的情书

亲爱的维克托:

多么希望我是个聪明的女人,多么希望我能够描绘你,我华丽的小鸟,你将美丽的外形、美丽的羽毛和美丽的歌声集于一身!

我要说你是所有时代里最伟大的奇迹,而我只是说出了这一事实。但是要用合适的词语表达这一点,我的完美的你,我得拥有比上天赋予我们同类的更为和谐的声音,因为我只是你最近嘲笑的卑下的猫头鹰,所以不能将你描绘。

我不会告诉你,你耀眼的程度,如你所知,你像具有甜蜜歌喉的小鸟依然美丽,令人称叹。

我很满意地将观看、倾听和羡慕的责任委任给它们,而对于我自己,我保留爱的权利,这可能听起来不那么顺耳,但对于内心,它要甜蜜得多。

我爱你,我爱你。我的维克托,我不能过多地重复这三个字,我无法表达我内心的感受。

我认识你所有的美——外形、颜色、香味以及和谐的声音,它们将我包围。你比什么都优秀,我看见并倾慕,你就是一切!

你不仅是有七种光色的太阳光谱,而且就是太阳本身,它照亮天宇,温暖万物,使世界生机勃勃。你就是这样,而我只是一个低微的女人,将你倾慕。

朱丽艾特
星期五晚上 8 点

① revivify [ri(:)'vivifai] v. 使再生,使振奋精神

14. Balzac's Love Letter to Evelina Hanska

奥诺·德·巴尔扎克(Honore de Balzac,1799~1850),法国作家和现实主义小说奠基人,他在作品集《人间喜剧》中描述了法国社会生活的全景。下面选辑的情书是他写给波兰女伯爵艾弗琳娜·汉斯卡(Evelina Hanska)的。

Sunday, 19th, June, 1836

My beloved angel,

I am nearly mad about you. I can no longer think of anything but you. My imagination always carries me to you. I grasp you, I kiss you, I caress① you.

As for my heart, there you will always be. I have a delicious sense of you there. But my God, what is to become of me, if you have deprived me of my imagination? This is a monomania② which, this morning terrifies me.

I rise up every moment saying to myself, "Come, I am going there!" Then I sit down again, moved by my imaginations. There is a frightful conflict I am confronted with. This is not life. I have never before been like that. You have devoured③ everything.

I feel foolish and happy as soon as I think of you. I whirl round in a delicious dream in which in one instant I live a thousand years. What a horrible situation!

I feel love in every pore, living only for love, and seeing myself

---

① caress [kə'res] v. 爱抚,接吻
② monomania [ˌmɔnəu'meinjə] n. 对一事的狂热,偏执狂
③ devour [di'vauə] v. 狼吞虎咽地吃

tormented① by grieves, and caught in a thousand spiders' threads.

O, my darling Eva②, you did not know it. I picked up your card. It is there before me, and I talk to you as if you were there. I see you, as I did yesterday, beautiful, astonishingly beautiful.

Yesterday, during the whole evening, I said to myself, "she is mine!" Ah! The angels are not as happy in Paradise as I was yesterday!

Honore

巴尔扎克致艾弗琳娜·汉斯卡的情书

我心爱的天使：

我几乎为你疯狂。除了你，我再也想不出他物，我的想象总是将我引向你。我要紧紧抱着你，吻你，抚慰你。

至于我的心，那儿是你的栖息地，那儿总可以美美地感觉你。但是，我的上帝，如果你剥夺了我的想象力，我会成为什么样子？今天早晨，这一偏执狂问题让我感到恐惧。

每个时刻，我都站起来对自己说："走吧，我要到那儿去！"然后坐下来，随着我的想象而去。我正面临可怕的斗争，这不是生活，我以前从不这样，你吞噬了我的一切。

一想到你，我就感到愚蠢而又快慰。我在甜美的梦中旋转，在那里，一瞬间，我度过了一千年，这是多么可怕的境况！

每一个气孔里都有爱的感觉，我只为爱而活着，看见了自己被痛苦折磨，似乎被一千只蜘蛛的线缠绕着。

啊！我亲爱的伊娃，你不知道这一切。我捡起你的名片，把它放在我面前，跟你诉说，好像它就是你，如同昨天一样，我又看见了你，那样美丽，那样惊艳。

昨天整个夜晚，我对自己说："她是我的！"啊！乐园里的天使也没有我昨天快乐！

奥诺
1836年6月19日星期日

---

① torment ['tɔːment] v. 使痛苦，折磨
② Eva ['iːvə] n. 对 Evelina 的昵称

15. Franz Liszt's Love Letters to Marie D'Agoult

弗朗兹·李斯特(Franz Liszt,1811~1886),匈牙利作曲家,一生中作为钢琴演奏家而闻名。他最著名的作品包括《但丁交响曲》(1856)和《浮士德交响曲》(1853~1861)。他在巴黎期间遇见了年轻貌美的已婚女伯爵玛丽·达高特(Marie D'Agoult)。她的婚姻很不幸福,并已与丈夫分居。她疯狂地爱上了李斯特。最后,他们结合在一起,成为夫妻。

I

Thursday morning 1834

Dear Marie,

My heart overflows with emotion and joy! I do not know what heavenly languor①, what infinite pleasure permeates② it and burns me up. It is as if I had never loved!!! Tell me whence these uncanny③ disturbances④ spring, these inexpressible foretastes⑤ of delight, these divine, tremors⑥ of love. Oh! All this can only spring from you, sister, angel, woman, Marie! All this can only be, is surely nothing less than a gentle ray streaming from your fiery soul, or else some secret poignant⑦ teardrop which you have long since left in my breast.

My God, my God, never force us apart, take pity on us! But what am I saying? Forgive my weakness, how

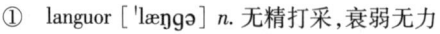

① languor [ˈlæŋgə] n. 无精打采,衰弱无力
② permeate [ˈpəːmieit] v. 弥漫,渗透,透过
③ uncanny [ʌnˈkæni] adj. 离奇的
④ disturbance [disˈtəːbəns] n. 骚动,动乱,打扰
⑤ foretaste [ˈfɔːteist] n. 预示
⑥ tremor [ˈtremə] n. 震动,颤动
⑦ poignant [ˈpɔignənt] adj. 令人痛苦的,辛辣的,剧烈的

couldst Thou① divide us! Thou wouldst have nothing but pity for us... No no! It is not in vain that our flesh and our souls quicken and become immortal② through Thy Word, which cries out deep within us Father, Father... out Thy hand to us, that our broken hearts seek their refuge in Thee... O! We thank, bless and praise Thee, O God, for all that Thou has given us, and all that Thou hast prepared for us....

This is to be—to be!

Marie! Marie!

Oh let me repeat that name a hundred times, a thousand times over; for three days now it has lived within me, oppressed me, set me afire. I am not writing to you, no, I am close beside you. I see you, I hear you. Eternity in your arms... Heaven, Hell, everything, all is within you, redoubled... Oh! Leave me free to rave in my delirium. Drab, tame, constricting reality is no longer enough for me. We must live our lives to the full, loving and suffering to extremes!

Franz

II

December 1834

Dear Marie,

Marie! Marie!

Oh let me repeat that name a hundred times, a thousand times over; for three days now it has lived within me, oppressed me, set me afire. I am not writing to you, no, I am close beside you.

I see you, I hear you... Eternity in your arms... Heaven, hell, all is within you and even more than all... Oh! Leave me free to rave③ in my delirium. Mean, cautious, narrow reality is no longer enough for me. We must live out lives to the full, our loves, our sorrow...! Oh! You believe

---

① couldst [kudst] 古体 can 的过去式;Thou:古体 you,这里特指"上帝",因而首字母大写。
② immortal [i'mɔːtl] adj. 不朽的
③ rave [reiv] v. 吼叫,发怒

me capable of self-sacrifice, chastity①, temperance② and piety③, do you not?

But let no more be said of this… it is for you to question, to draw conclusions, to save me as you see fit. Let me be mad, senseless since you can do nothing, nothing at all for me. It is good for me to speak to you now. This is to be! To be!!!

Franz

弗朗兹·李斯特致玛丽·达高特的情书

其 一

亲爱的玛丽:

感情和欢乐在我心中泛滥！我不知道是什么样的美妙柔情,是什么样的无穷快乐渗透了我的心,将我燃烧。似乎我从没有爱过!!!告诉我,这些奇异的躁动,这些难以形容的欢乐征兆,这些神圣的爱的振动是从那里一跃而出。啊！这一切只是从你身上跃出,我的妹妹,我的天使,我的女人,玛丽！这一切只会是,也肯定只是从你火热的灵魂里射出的温柔光线,或者是你长期留在我胸腔里的,某种秘密的、辛酸的泪珠。

我的上帝,我的上帝,千万不要将我们分开,可怜可怜我们！我说了什么？请原谅我的软弱,您怎么会将我们分开！您只会对我们充满同情……不,不！您的话语肯定有益于加速我们的肉体和灵魂变得永恒,它就在我们身体里面呼唤。上帝,上帝！将您的手伸给我们,我们破碎的心在您那里寻求避难……啊！上帝,我们歌颂您,感谢您给了我们的以及为我们准备的这一切……

就是这,就这！

玛丽！玛丽！

啊,让我一百遍、一千遍重复这个名

---

① chastity [ˈtʃæstiti] n. 纯洁,贞节
② temperance [ˈtempərəns] n. 节欲,戒酒
③ piety [ˈpaiəti] n. 虔诚,孝行

字,它在我的心里呆了三天,压迫着我,让我火烧火燎。我不是在给你写信,不,我在靠近你。我看着你,听着你。永恒在你的怀中……天堂、地狱、一切一切在你身体里面,并成倍增长……啊!让我自由地、欣喜若狂地高声大喊。单调的、驯服的、限制人的现实再也不能满足我。我们要活得充分,要爱到极点,痛苦到极点。

弗朗兹
1834年星期四早晨

其　　二

亲爱的玛丽:

　　玛丽!玛丽!

　　啊,让我一百遍、一千遍重复这个名字,它在我的心里呆了三天,压迫着我,让我火烧火燎。我不是在给你写信,不,我在靠近你。

　　我看着你,听着你。永恒在你的怀中……天堂、地狱、一切一切在你身体里面,甚至还有更多。啊!让我自由地、欣喜若狂地高声大喊。吝啬的、谨慎的、狭窄的现实再也不能满足我。我们要活得充分,我们的爱,我们的痛苦……啊!你相不相信我能够牺牲自我、保持贞洁、克制欲望以及拥有虔诚?

　　但是,别再提这些了……你可以提问,得出结论,如果你觉得合适,请你拯救我!如果你为我什么都做不了,那就让我疯狂,失去理智。我现在对你说这些会更好,就是这!就这!!!

弗朗兹
1834年12月

16. Robert Schumann's Love Letter to Clara Wieck

罗伯特·舒曼(Robert Schumann, 1810~1856), 17世纪德国著名的作曲家和钢琴家, 他以创作歌剧和钢琴曲而闻名于世。他师从弗里德里克·维克(Friederich Wieck)时爱上了老师的女儿克拉拉·维克(Clara Wieck), 他们的爱情遭到了老师的坚决反对。舒曼坚持要娶克拉拉, 其决心之大, 以至于他诉之法庭, 寻求法律帮助。他的爱最终取得了胜利。

1838

Clara,

How happy your last letters have made me—those since Christmas Eve! I should like to call you by all the endearing epithets①, and yet I can find no lovelier word than the simple word "dear", but there is a particular way of saying it. My dear one, then, I have wept for joy to think that you are mine, and often wonder if I deserve you.

One would think that no one man's heart and brain could stand all the things that are crowded into one day. Where do these thousands of thoughts, wishes, sorrows, joys and hopes come from? Day in, day out, the procession goes on. But how light-hearted I was yesterday and the day before! There shone out of your letters so noble a spirit, such faith, such a wealth of love!

What should I do for love of you, my own Clara? The knights of old were good examples; they could go through fire or slay dragons to win their ladies, but we of today have to content ourselves with more prosaic② methods, such as smoking fewer cigars, and the like. After all, though, we can love, knights or no knights; and so,

---

① epithet ['epiθet] *n.* 表述词语, 绰号, 称号
② prosaic [prəu'zeiik] *adj.* 散文的, 散文体的, 平凡的

as ever, only the times change, not men's hearts…

You cannot think how your letter has raised and strengthened me! You are splendid, and I am quite proud of you. I have made up my mind to read all your wishes in your face. Then you will think, even though you don't say it, that your Robert is a really good sort, that he is entirely yours, and he loves you more than words can say. You shall indeed have cause to think so in the happy future. I still see you as you looked in your little cap that last evening. I still hear you call me.

But I see you in many another unforgettable guise①. Once you were in a black dress, going to the theatre; it was during our separation. I know you will not have forgotten; it is vivid with me. Another time you were walking in the Thomasgasschen② with an umbrella up, and you avoided me in desperation. And yet another time, as you were putting on your hat after a concert, our eyes happened to meet, and yours were full of the old unchanging love.

I picture you in all sorts of ways, as I have seen you since. I did not look at you much, but you charmed me so immeasurably… Ah, I can never praise you enough for yourself or for your love of me, which I don't really deserve.

Robert

罗伯特·舒曼致克拉拉·维克的情书

克拉拉：

　　你平安夜之后写来的几封信真让我高兴！我真想用所有亲密的爱称来呼唤你，可是，我找不出比"亲爱的"这简单的称呼更甜的字眼了，但要用特别的方式说出来。我的亲爱的，一想到你是我的，我就欣喜得直流泪，并常常怀疑自己是不是值得你爱。

　　人们会想，没有一个人的心和脑承受得起一天之内涌入的这么多的信息。这些成千上万的想法、愿望、痛苦、欢欣和希望是从哪里来的？日出日

---

① guise [gaiz] n. 外观、姿态、装束
② Thomasgasschen　托马斯加臣剧院

落,这些东西继续涌入。昨天和前天,我感到非常舒畅!你的信中闪烁着多么崇高的精神和信念以及多么丰富的爱!

　　为了你的爱,我的克拉拉,我该做些什么?古时候的骑士就是个好榜样,他们为了赢得女人的爱可以下火海或杀死凶暴的火龙,而今天的我们却以异常平凡的方式自我满足,比如少抽些烟,等等。然而,不管我们是不是骑士,我们毕竟也能去爱,所以,像以前一样,只是时代变了,男人的心没有变……

　　你想象不出你的信如何使我神采飞扬、精力充沛,你真是奇妙,我非常为你感到骄傲。我下定了决心,要读懂你脸上所有的愿望。然后,即使你不说出来,你也会认为你的罗伯特真是好样的,他完全属于你,他对你的爱无法用语言形容。在幸福的未来,你肯定有理由这样想。你昨晚戴着小帽子的样子依然浮现在我眼前,你呼唤我的声音也在耳边。

　　但我也看见你许多其他梳妆打扮的模样。有一次,你穿着一身黑衣服上剧院,那时正值我们分手,我知道你不会忘记,那个样子在我的脑海里依然栩栩如生。另一次,你打着伞走进托马斯加臣剧院,你失望地躲着我。还有一次,音乐会结束后,你戴上帽子,我们的眼神碰巧相遇,你的眼里充满了古老不变的情愫。

　　我想象得出你在我们相识之后的所有的样子,我不曾多看你,但你的魅力无法比拟。啊,我没有足够的词语来称赞你本人以及你对我的爱,而我真的不配你对我的爱。

罗伯特
1838 年

17. Stowe's Love Letter to Her Husband

1852年,哈里特·比契·斯托写出了《汤姆叔叔的小屋》,立刻获得了巨大的成功,同时也招来了不少非议。她出版了八部长篇小说和数十篇短篇小说。她喜欢和丈夫凯文以及六个孩子过着幸福忙碌的家庭生活。这封信是她婚后第十一年写的,表达了她和丈夫共享的喜怒哀乐。

January 1, 1847

My Dearest Husband,

    I was at that date of marriage a very different being from what I am now and stood in relation to my Heavenly Father in a very different attitude. My whole desire was to live in love, absorbing passionate① devotion to one person. Our separation was my first trial—but then came a note of comfort in the hope of being a mother. No creature ever so longed to see the face of a little one or had such a heart full of love to bestow②. Here came in trial again sickness, pain, perplexity③, constant discouragement—wearing wasting days and nights—husband gone… When you came back you came only to increasing perplexities.

    Ah, how little comfort I had in being a mother—how was all that I proposed met and crossed and my youth may ever be hedged up!

    In short, God would teach me that I should make no family be my chief good and portion and bitter as the lesson has been I thank Him for it from my very soul. One might naturally infer that from the

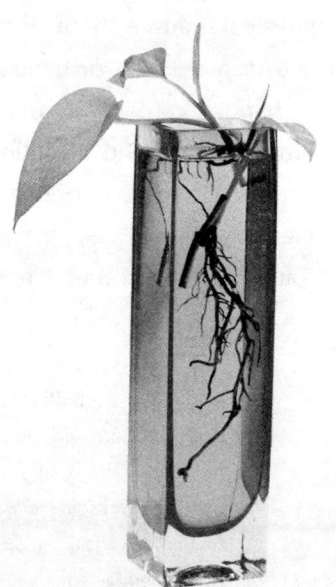

---

①   passionate ['pæʃənit] *adj.* 充满热情的
②   bestow [bi'stəu] *v.* 给予,安放
③   perplexity [pə'pleksiti] *n.* 困惑混乱

union of two both morbidly① sensitive and acute②, yet in many respects exact opposites—one hasty and impulsive③—the other sensitive and brooding—one the very personification of exactness and routine and the other to whom everything of the kind was an irksome④ effort—from all this what should one infer but some painful friction⑤.

But all this would not after all have done so very much had not Providence as if intent to try us throws upon the heaviest external pressure… but still where you have failed your faults have been to me those of one beloved—of the man who after all would be the choice of my heart still were I to choose—for were I now free I should again love just as I did and again feel that I could give up all to and for you—and if I do not love never can love again with the blind and unwise love with which I married I love quite as truly tho far more wisely…

In reflecting upon our future union—our marriage—the past obstacles to our happiness—it seems to me that they are of two or three kinds. First, those from physical causes both in you and in me—such on your part

as hypochondriac⑥ morbid instability for which the only remedy is physical care and attention to the laws of health—and on my part an excess of sensitiveness and of confusion and want of control of mind and memory. This always increases on my part in proportion as I blamed and found fault with and I hope will decrease with returning health. I hope

---

① morbidly [ˈmɔːbidli] *adv.* 病态地
② acute [əˈkjuːt] *adj.* 敏锐的
③ impulsive [imˈpʌlsiv] *adj.* 冲动的
④ irksome [ˈəːksəm] *adj.* 令人厌恶的,讨厌的
⑤ friction [ˈfrikʃən] *n.* 摩擦,摩擦力
⑥ hypochondriac [ˌhaipəuˈkɔndriæk] *adj.* 忧郁症的

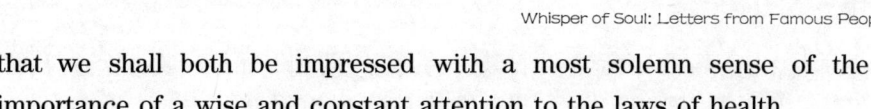

that we shall both be impressed with a most solemn sense of the importance of a wise and constant attention to the laws of health.

Then in the second place the want of any definite plan of mutual① watchfulness, with regard to each other's improvement, of a definite time and place for doing it with a firm determination to improve and be improved by each other—to confess our faults one to another and pray one for another that we may be healed…

Yours with much love
H.

斯托致丈夫的情书

我最亲爱的夫君：

结婚那天的我与现在相比，判若两人；与昔日相比，我和天父的关系也有了改变。我全部的愿望就是生活在爱的包围圈，全心全意地去爱一个人。我们的分离是我的第一次考验——但不久就要做母亲的期待给我带来一丝安慰。没有人会像我一样渴望看到那张可爱的小脸，心中被即将给予的爱意溢满。接着又有疾病、痛苦、困惑、挫折的考验——虚度过的日日夜夜让人疲惫不堪——丈夫离开了……而你的到来只会增加困惑忙乱。

唉，做母亲的快乐让我享受得实在太少——我所预想的一切怎么就交织在一起？我的青春怎么就被圈进了篱笆？

总之，上帝让我懂得，我不应该为家庭的琐细主宰我的幸福悲戚，我打心里对他感激。人们很自然地猜测这样的两个人的结合应是何种结果。我们两个都忧郁、敏感——而在许多方面却完全相反——一个急躁、冲动；另一个敏感、忧虑；一个按部就班，另一个则觉得如此精致却让人厌烦——由此看来，人们应推测出我们痛苦的摩擦根源。

假若上帝还未有意给予我们最沉重的外在压力，一切还未变得如此糟糕……可是，那

---

① mutual [ˈmjuːtjuəl] adj. 相互的

些缺点你仍没有改掉,那曾在我爱过的人身上找到。如果让我再次选择,你仍然是我心中的理想伴侣,如果现在我是自由之身,让我再次去爱,我仍然会如往昔般爱你,愿意为你放弃一切,给你我的所有,如果我不会这么盲目愚蠢地爱着和我结婚的人,我对你的爱可能会更加明智……

说到我们将来的结合——我们的婚姻——我们过去的幸福的障碍,对我而言,似乎有其二三:第一是你和我身体上的原因,比如你的忧郁症和病态的不稳定,唯一的治疗办法就是细心的照料和对健康的关注,还有我过度的敏感,思维混乱,心智和记忆缺乏控制。这些总让我抱怨、挑剔。我希望随着健康的不断好转,我们这些症状将会改善。我还希望我们都能认识到健康的重要性,并不断加以关注。

第二点就是没有一个具体的计划互相监督双方的进步,没有具体的时间、地点和坚定的决心来提高和帮助对方提高,向对方承认彼此的缺点并祈祷对方康复……

深爱你的
H
1847年1月1日

18. Flaubert's Love Letter to Louise Colet

古斯塔夫·福楼拜(Gustave Flaubert, 1821~1880), 法国著名作家, 被认为是自然主义学说的先驱, 以严谨的文风著称。他的著作包括《包法利夫人》(Madame Bovary, 1857)和短篇小说《纯朴的心》(A Simple Heart, 1877), 以下情书是他写给妻子路易莎·古内(Louise Colet)的。

August 21, 1853

Dear Louise,

Have you really not noticed, then, that here of all places, in this private, personal solitude① that surrounds me, I have turned to you? All the memories of my youth speak to me as I walk, just as the seashells crunch under my feet on the beach. The crash of every wave awakens far-distant reverberations② within me.

I hear the rumble of bygone days, and in my mind the whole endless series of old passions surges forward like the billows③. I remember my spasms④, my sorrows, gusts of desire that whistled like wind in the rigging, and vast vague longings that swirled in the dark like a flock of wild gulls in a storm cloud.

On whom should I lean, if not on you? My weary mind turns for refreshment⑤ to the thought of you as a dusty traveler might sink onto a soft and grassy bank.

Gustave

---

① solitude ['sɔlitjuːd] n. 孤独
② reverberation [riˌvəːbə'reiʃən] n. 反响, 回响
③ billow ['biləu] n. 巨浪
④ spasm ['spæzəm] n. 一阵发作, 痉挛
⑤ refreshment [ri'freʃmənt] n. 精力恢复, 点心

福楼拜致路易莎·古内的情书

亲爱的路易莎：

　　你是否真的没有注意？那时，这里所有的地方，一种内心的孤寂缠绕着我，就在这当中，我总是想到你。散步时，我年轻时所有的记忆袭上心头，就像海滩上的贝壳在脚下被踩得吱吱作响。每一次海浪的爆裂声都唤醒我心中遥远的回声。

　　我听见以往岁月的隆隆声，在我的脑海里，这些无穷无尽的古老激情像巨浪一样向前翻腾。我记得我的内心痉挛、我的忧伤、像海风刮过船桅发出呼呼声的阵阵欲望，以及宽广无边却又模模糊糊的渴望，像暴风雨来临，乌云遮蔽的天空下，一群野鸥在黑暗中盘旋。

　　如果不是你的话，我该靠着谁呢？一想起你，我疲惫的头脑顿时感到神清气爽，就像满身尘土的游子躺在长满青草的柔软的河岸上。

古斯塔夫
1853 年 8 月 21 日

19. Mark Twain's Love Letter to Olivia Langdon

马克·吐温(Mark Twain, 1835~1910), 美国作家, 本名为 Samuel Langhorne Clemens, 他曾回顾其密西西比河边的童年时光, 创作了杰出的幽默和讽刺小说, 包括《汤姆·索耶历险记》(1876)和《哈克贝利·费恩历险记》(1884)。以下选辑的是他给未来的妻子奥利维亚·兰敦(Olivia Langdon)写的情书。

May 12, 1869

Dear Olivia,

  Out of the depths of my happy heart wells a great tide of love and prayer for this priceless treasure that is confided to① my life-long keeping.

  You cannot see its intangible② waves as they flow towards you, darling, but in these lines you will hear, as it were, the distant beating of the surf.

Sam

马克·吐温致奥利维亚·兰敦的情书

亲爱的奥利维亚:

  在我幸福的内心深处蕴藏着巨大的爱情潮水,我为这一终身保存的无价之宝而祈祷。

  你看不见我的爱掀起无形的波浪向你涌去,亲爱的,但是,在字里行间,你会听见像往常一样遥远的海浪拍击声。

萨姆
1869 年 5 月 12 日

---

① be confided to 把……委托给
② intangible [in'tændʒəbl] adj. 不可捉摸的,难以明白的

20. Mark Twain's Letters to Mrs. Jane Clemens and Family

  1847年父亲去世后,马克·吐温开始自谋生计。当过排字工人、领航员和水手,并找过金矿,后在弗吉尼亚城当记者。1863年始用马克·吐温笔名写作。1865年发表成名处女作《卡拉维拉斯县著名的跳蛙》。同年开始游历,发表50多篇报道。1869年发表《老实人在国外》,嘲讽资产阶级的愚蠢行为。1893年先后访问非、欧、亚、澳洲各地。以下选编的两封信就是在他游历期间给家人写的。

I

Westminster Hotel, New York
June 1, 1867

Dear Folks,

  I know I ought to write oftener and more fully, but I cannot overcome my repugnance① to telling what I am doing or what I expect to do or propose to do. Then, what have I left to write about? Manifestly② nothing.

  It isn't any use for me to talk about the voyage, because I can have no faith in that voyage till the ship is under way. How do I know she will ever sail? My passage is paid, and if the ship sails, I sail in her—but I make no calculations, have bought no cigars, no sea-going clothing—have made no preparation whatever—shall not pack my trunk till the morning we sail. Yet my hands are full of what I am going to do the day before we sail—and what isn't done that day will go undone.

  All I do know or feel, is, that I am wild with impatience to move—move—move! Half a dozen times I have wished I had sailed long ago in some ship that wasn't going to keep

---

① repugnance [ri'pʌgnəns] *n.* 不一致
② manifestly ['mænifestli] *adv.* 明白地

me chained here to chafe for lagging① ages while she got ready to go. Curse the endless delays! They always kill me—they make me neglect every duty and then I have a conscience② that tears me like a wild beast.

I wish I never had to stop anywhere a month. I do more mean things, the moment I get a chance to fold my hands and sit down than ever I can get forgiveness for.

Yes, we are to meet at Mr. Beach's next Thursday night, and I suppose we shall have to be gotten up regardless of expense, in swallow-tails, white kids and everything en regle③.

I am resigned to Rev. Mr. Hutchinson's or anybody else's supervision④. I don't mind it. I am fixed. I have got a splendid, immoral, tobacco-smoking, wine-drinking, godless room-mate who is as good and true and right-minded a man as ever lived—a man whose blameless conduct and example will always be an eloquent⑤ sermon to all who shall come within their influence. But send on the professional preachers—there are none I like better to converse⑥ with. If they're not narrow-minded and bigoted they make good companions.

I asked them to send the N. Y. Weekly to you—no charge. I am not going to write for it. Like all other papers that pay one splendidly it circulates among stupid people and the "canaille"⑦. I have made no arrangement with any New York paper—I will see about that Monday or Tuesday. Love to all, Good bye!

Yours affectionately
Sam

～～～～～～～～～～

① lagging [ˈlægiŋ] adj. 最后的
② conscience [ˈkɔnʃəns] n. 良心,道德心
③ en regle [法语]按照规定,按照程序
④ supervision [ˌsjuːpəˈviʒən] n. 监督,管理
⑤ eloquent [ˈeləkwənt] adj. 雄辩的,有口才的
⑥ converse [kənˈvɔːs] v. 谈话,交谈
⑦ canaille [kəˈneili] n. 暴民,贱民

II

Yalta, Russia
Aug. 25, 1867

Dear Folks,

    We have been representing the United States. We went to Sebastopol①, after we got tired of Constantinople②（got your letter there, and one at Naples）and there the Commandant and the whole town came aboard and were as jolly③ and sociable④ as old friends. They said the Emperor of Russia was at Yalta⑤, 30 miles or 40 away, and urged us to go there with the ship and visit him—promised us a cordial welcome. They insisted on sending a telegram to the Emperor, and also a courier overland to announce our coming. But we knew that a great English Excursion party, and also the Viceroy of Egypt, in his splendid yacht⑥, had been refused an audience within the last fortnight, so we thought it not safe to try it. They said, no difference—the Emperor would hardly visit our ship, because that would be a most extraordinary favor, and one which he uniformly refuses to accord under any circumstances, but he would certainly receive us at his palace. We still declined. But we had to go to Odessa, 250 miles away, and there the Governor General urged us, and sent a telegram to the Emperor, which we hardly expected to be

---

① Sebastopol [si'bæstəpɔl] 塞瓦斯托波尔,俄罗斯克里米亚半岛西南岸港市。
② Constantinople [ˌkɔnstænti'nəupl] 君士坦丁堡,土耳其西北部港市。
③ jolly ['dʒɔli] *adj.* 欢乐的
④ sociable ['səuʃəbl] *adj.* 好交际的,友善的
⑤ Yalta ['jæltə] 雅尔塔,俄罗斯西南欧部分一城市,位于黑海沿岸、克里米亚南部,是一个受欢迎的旅游胜地,也是1945年2月同盟国会议的会址所在地。
⑥ yacht [jɔt] *n.* 游艇,快艇

answered, but it was, and promptly. So we sailed back to Yalta.

We all went to the palace at noon, today, (3 miles) in carriages and on horses sent by the Emperor, and we had a jolly time. Instead of the usual formal audience of 15 minutes, we stayed 4 hours and were made a good deal more at home than we could have been in a New York drawing-room. The whole tribe turned out to receive our party—Emperor, Empress, the oldest daughter (Grand-Duchess Marie, a pretty girl of 14,) a little Grand Duke, her brother, and a platoon of Admirals, Princes, Peers of the Empire, etc., and in a little while an aid-de-camp① arrived with a request from the Grand Duke Michael, the Emperor's brother, that we would visit his palace and breakfast with him.  The Emperor also invited us, on behalf of his absent eldest son and heir (aged 22), to visit his palace and consider it a visit to him. They all talk English and they were all very neatly but very plainly dressed. You all dress a good deal finer than they were dressed. The Emperor and his family threw off all reserve and showed us all over the palace themselves. It is very rich and very elegant, but in no way gaudy②.

I had been appointed chairman of a committee to draught an address to the Emperor in behalf of③ the passengers, and as I fully expected, and as they fully intended, I had to write the address myself. I didn't mind it, because I have no modesty and would as soon write to an Emperor as to anybody else—but considering that there were 5 on the committee I thought they might have contributed one paragraph among them, anyway. They wanted me to read it to him, too, but I declined④ that

① aid-de-camp 侍从官, 副官
② gaudy [ˈɡɔːdi] adj. 华而不实的
③ in behalf of 代表
④ decline [diˈklain] v. 拒绝

honor—not because I hadn't cheek enough (and some to spare,) but because our Consul at Odessa was along, and also the Secretary of our Legation at St. Petersburgh, and of course one of those ought to read it.

The Emperor accepted the address—it was his business to do it—and so many others have praised it warmly that I begin to imagine it must be a wonderful sort of document and herewith send you the original draught of it to be put into alcohol and preserved forever like a curious reptile①.

They live right well at the Grand Duke Michael's—their breakfasts are not gorgeous② but very excellent—and if Mike were to say the word I would go there and breakfast with him tomorrow.

Yours affectionately
Sam

P. S. They had told us it would be polite to invite the Emperor to visit the ship, though he would not be likely to do it. But he didn't give us a chance—he has requested permission to come on board with his family and all his relations tomorrow and take a sail, in case it is calm weather. I can entertain them. My hand is in, now, and if you want any more Emperors feted in style, trot them out.

---

① reptile [ˈreptail] n. 爬行动物
② gorgeous [ˈgɔːdʒəs] adj. 华丽的,灿烂的

马克·吐温致夫人及家人

其　一

亲爱的家人：

　　我知道我应该更经常地给你们写信，内容更加充分，但我十分不愿意描述我在做什么，希望做什么或打算做什么。那么，我还有什么要写的呢？显然无话可说。

　　谈论这次航行对我毫无用处，因为直到船开了我才会相信真的要起航。我怎么知道它会不会起航？有人为我买了船票，要是轮船起程，我就坐在船上随船航行。但我什么都没有准备，没有买雪茄，没有买出海穿的衣服，直到早上船要开了才去整理旅行箱。开船前一天我手边还有很多活儿要做，直到离开还没做完。

　　我只知道或感觉到，我一直疯狂地想着出发，出发，出发！不知道有多少次希望我一早儿就已经出海了，而不是被困在这儿蹉跎岁月，等船准备停当。该死的没完没了的耽搁！耽搁总让我发疯，让我什么都不想做，我有一种责任感，像一头野兽在撕扯着我。

　　真希望我不会在任何地方停留一个月。当我有机会坐下来双手合十忏悔的时候，我会做更多普通的事情。

　　当然，下周四晚我们要在比奇先生家碰面，我猜我们一定会不在乎花销多大，都要穿燕尾服，把孩子们收拾得干净整齐，让一切都迥然有序。

　　我被安排和哈钦森牧师或其他什么人一起住，但我不管这些，我已经安顿好了。我的室友不同凡响，放荡不羁，吸烟喝酒，不信神灵，友好真诚，头脑清晰，他的行为举止无可指责，对于那些受其影响的人来说无异于一次雄辩的布道，但那些靠布道吃饭的牧师们，没有一个我喜欢与其交谈的。如果不那么心胸狭隘，不那么固执偏见，他们倒还是不错的旅伴。

　　我让他们免费寄送《纽约周报》给你们。我不准备再给《纽约周报》写东西了。像所有其他稿酬丰厚的报纸一样,《纽约周报》只给蠢人和"贱民"看。我和纽约的任何报纸都没有安排——我周一或周二安排一下,爱你们所有人,再见!

爱你们的
萨姆
1867年6月1日
于纽约威斯特明斯特宾馆

其　二

亲爱的家人:

我们一直代表着美国。我们厌倦了君士坦丁堡(在那里收到你们的信,还有在那不勒斯的一封)之后,就去了塞瓦斯托波尔,在那里边防司令和整个镇的人都上了我们的船,他们像老朋友一样愉快随和。他们说俄罗斯皇帝在三四十英里外的雅尔塔,敦促我们乘船去那儿拜访他——并保证说皇帝一定会热烈欢迎我们。他们坚持要给皇帝发电报,并且派通讯员去通知我们的到来。但我们知道曾经有一个不错的英国旅行团,还有埃及总督,乘着豪华的游艇,在前两周内都被拒绝接见,因此我们认为这一举动不太靠谱。他们说,没有关系——皇帝十有八九不会拜访我们的船队,因为那是个极大的恩宠,在任何情况下他都不会去做的;然而他会在他的宫殿接见我们。我们仍然婉言谢绝了,但是我们必须去250英里外的敖德萨,那里的总督催促我们,并且给皇帝发了一份我们几乎不期望有回复的电报——但是很快就得到了回复,因此我们返回了雅尔塔。

今天中午我们骑着皇帝派来的马或乘着马车去了宫殿,有三英里的路程,在那里过得很愉快。本来是寻常的15分钟正式接见,我们却谈了4个

小时,并且比在纽约的会客厅里谈得还投机得多。整个皇族——皇帝、皇后、他们最大的女儿玛丽公爵(一个漂亮的14岁女孩)、她弟弟小公爵,还有一群舰队司令、王子、皇宫贵族,等等——都乐于接见我们这个小团队。过了一会儿,一个随从参谋带来了大公爵迈克尔的请求,迈克尔是皇帝的弟弟,我们将会去拜访他,并同他一道吃早餐。皇帝的22岁的长子,也是继承人,今天没有来,皇帝就代表他邀请

心灵的私语

Whisper of Soul: Letters from Famous People

我们访问他的宫殿，他们用英语交谈，衣着朴素但非常整齐，你们穿的比他们好多了。皇帝和他的家人抛开所有的预约亲自带领我们参观宫殿，宫殿富丽堂皇但绝不绚丽。

我已经被任命为委员会主席，代表这个团队给皇帝致辞，正如我期望的和他们打算的那样，我得亲自动手写这个东西。我不介意，不谦虚地说，我将会像给其他人写信一样很快写给皇帝。但因为委员会有五个人，所以我想这里面大概有一段是他们的成绩。他们想让我把它读给皇帝，但我谢绝了那个荣誉，不是因为我面子不够（还要留些面子），而是因为我们在敖德萨的领事和在圣匹兹堡的公使馆人员的秘书都在，应该是他们中某一位读它。

皇帝接受了我的致辞，这是他的职责所在。很多人都热烈称赞这篇东西，于是我相信它一定很不错，随同此信把原稿寄给你们，你们一定要好好保存，像保存一条稀奇古怪的蛇一样，把它放在酒精里。

他们住在大公爵迈克尔的家，早餐不是很丰盛但很好，如果迈克尔邀请的话，我明天要去那儿和他共进早餐。

爱你们的
萨姆
1867年8月25日
于俄国雅尔塔

附：他们告诉我们，邀请皇帝去参观船舰会是很礼貌的举动，尽管他不愿意。但是我们没有邀请的机会——他已经申请并被允许和家人及亲戚一起登船远航（如果天气好的话）。我会好好招待他们——现在已经开始准备了。如果你想不落俗套地款待皇帝，就奉承他们。

21. Mark Twain's Letter to Orion Clemens

马克·吐温本有兄弟姐妹 7 人,但只有哥哥奥里恩、姐姐帕梅拉和他活到了成年。1851 年,他来到哥哥的印刷厂当排字工人。1856 年去新奥尔良,后在密西西比河做舵手。以下是他带着母亲和姐姐出外旅游时给哥哥写的信。

ST. LOUIS
March, 1860

My Dear Brother,

  Your last letter has just come to hand. It reminds me strongly of Tom Hood's letters to his family, (which I have been reading lately). But yours only remind me of his, for although there is a striking likeness, your humor is much finer than his, and far better expressed. Tom Hood's wit, (in his letters) has a savor of labor about it which is very disagreeable.

  Your letter is good. That portion of it wherein the old sow figures is the very best thing I have seen lately. Its quiet style resembles Goldsmith's① "Citizen of the World", and "Don Quixote②", —which are my beau ideals of fine writing.

  You have paid the preacher! Well, that is good, also. What a man wants with religion in these breadless times, surpasses my comprehension③.

  Pamela and I have just returned from a visit to the most

---

  ① Oliver Goldsmith 奥利弗·戈德史密斯(1728~1774),英国作家,他在文学界的名声主要归功于他的小说《威克菲尔德的牧师》(The Vicar of Wakefield,1766 年)。

  ② Don Quixote [dɔnˈkwiksət] 堂吉诃德,西班牙作家塞万提斯(Cervantes)所著同名小说及其主人公。

  ③ comprehension [ˌkɔmpriˈhenʃən] n. 理解,包含

wonderfully beautiful painting which this city has ever seen—Church's① "Heart of the Andes"—which represents a lovely valley with its rich vegetation in all the bloom and glory of a tropical② summer—dotted with birds and flowers of all colors and shades of color, and sunny slopes, and shady corners, and twilight③ groves④, and cool cascades⑤—all grandly set off with a majestic⑥ mountain in the background with its gleaming summit clothed in everlasting ice and snow! I have seen it several times, but it is always a new picture—totally new—you seem to see nothing the second time which you saw the first.

We took the opera glass, and examined its beauties minutely, for the naked eye cannot discern the little wayside flowers, and soft shadows and patches of sunshine, and half-hidden bunches of grass and jets of water which form some of its most enchanting⑦ features. There is no slurring of perspective effect about it—the most distant—the minutest object in it has a marked and distinct personality—so that you may count the very leaves on the trees. When you first see the tame, ordinary-looking picture, your first impulse is to turn your back upon it, and say "Humbug"—but your third visit will find your brain gasping and straining with futile efforts to take all the wonder in—and appreciate it in its fullness—and understand how such a miracle could have been conceived and executed by human brain and human hands. You will never get tired

---

① Frederick Edwin Church 弗雷德里克·埃德温·丘奇(1826~1900)，美国画家，哈得孙河派的领袖。
② tropical ['trɔpikl] adj. 热带的，热情的
③ twilight ['twailait] n. 黎明，微光
④ grove [grəuv] n. 小树林
⑤ cascade [kæs'keid] n. 小瀑布
⑥ majestic [mə'dʒestik] adj. 宏伟的，庄严的
⑦ enchanting [in'tʃɑːntiŋ] adj. 迷人的，迷惑的，妩媚的

of looking at the picture, but your reflections—your efforts to grasp an intelligible① Something—you hardly know what—will grow so painful that you will have to go away from the thing, in order to obtain relief. You may find relief, but you cannot banish the picture—It remains with you still. It is in my mind now—and the smallest feature could not be removed without my detecting it. So much for the "Heart of the Andes".

Ma was delighted with her trip, but she was disgusted with the girls for allowing me to embrace and kiss them—and she was horrified at the Schottische② as performed by Miss Castle and myself. She was perfectly willing for me to dance until 12 o'clock at the imminent③ peril of my going to sleep on the after watch—but then she would top off with a very inconsistent④ sermon on dancing in general; ending with a terrific broadside aimed at that heresy⑤ of heresies, the Schottische.

I took Ma and the girls in a carriage, round that portion of New Orleans where the finest gardens and residences are to be seen, and although it was a blazing hot dusty day, they seemed hugely delighted. To use an expression which is commonly ignored in polite society, they were "hell-bent" on stealing some of the luscious⑥-looking oranges from branches which overhung the fences, but I restrained⑦ them. They were not aware before that shrubbery could be made to take any queer shape which a skilful gardener might choose to twist it into, so they found not only beauty but novelty in their visit. We went out to Lake Pontchartrain in the cars.

Your Brother
Sam Clemens

① intelligible [in'telidʒəbl] adj. 可理解的
② Schottische [ʃɔ'tiːʃ] n. 慢步波尔卡舞曲的一种
③ imminent ['iminənt] adj. 即将来临的,逼近的
④ inconsistent [ˌinkən'sistənt] adj. 不一致的,不协调的
⑤ heresy ['herəsi] n. 异端,异教
⑥ luscious ['lʌʃəs] adj. 甘美的
⑦ restrain [ris'trein] v. 抑制,制止

马克·吐温致奥里恩·克莱门斯

我亲爱的哥哥：

你的上一封信刚刚到达我手中，它使我强烈地想起汤姆·胡德的家书（最近我正在读那本书）。但仅仅是想起了他而已，因为虽然你们有惊人的相似之处，但是你比他更幽默，并且也远远比他表达得流畅。汤姆·胡德的机智（在他的家书中）不太自然，让人生厌。

你的信很不错，关于播种老农的那部分是我近来读过的最好的描述。闲适的风格很像戈德史密斯的《世界公民》，还有《堂吉诃德》——它们是我看过的最优秀的作品。

你已经付钱给那位牧师了，这样也不错。在这个物质匮乏的时代，一个人需要从宗教那里得到的东西远远超过了我的理解。

我和帕米拉刚刚去看过一幅精美绝伦的油画，它在这座城市里已经展览过，丘奇的《安第斯山之心》，画的是一个可爱的山谷，正是热带的夏季，到处郁郁葱葱，飞鸟和各色的花朵处处可见，斜坡阳光灿烂，角落被树阴所盖，小树林光线昏暗，瀑布凉爽宜人——画面的背景是雄壮的山脉，微微发光的山顶被经年不化的冰雪所覆盖。我看过它好几次了，常看常新，上一次看到的东西下一次再不会看到。我们拿着看歌剧时戴的望远镜，仔细观察它的美丽之处。因为肉眼无法分辨出道路两旁的小花，柔弱的阴影和光斑，若隐若现的草丝和水的急流——这些都构成了画中最迷人的景

象。它没有模糊的透视效果——最远的——最微缩的物体都有明显而又截然不同的品格，你甚至可以数清树上的叶子。第一次看到这幅平静而普通的画，你会立刻背过身去，说"什么玩意儿啊"，但第三次看它时，你就会发现大脑似乎在喘息，徒劳地想把这个奇妙的东西装进去，享受它，弄明白这么一个奇迹是怎样被人类的双手和大脑创造出来的。你会不知疲倦地盯着这幅画看，但你的反应——你想去抓住什么可以明白的东西——你几乎不知道是什么东西让你如此痛苦，痛苦得让你不得不摆脱它。你可以解脱，但你不能摆脱这幅画，它仍在你脑海中浮现。反正现在它在我脑子里，每个细节

都清清楚楚。——关于《安第斯山之心》就说到这儿吧。

　　妈妈在旅行中很快乐,但是她很反感那些姑娘允许我拥抱并亲吻她们。她还十分厌恶卡赛尔小姐和我表演的慢步舞曲。她很乐意我跳舞跳到12点,直到转钟时刻我快昏昏欲睡为止,然后她总会对跳舞做一个总的、很不融洽的评价,猛烈抨击这个异端中的异端,即慢步舞曲。

　　我带妈妈和姑娘们坐着马车,绕着新奥尔良一些地方转了一下,不久那里就会建起漂亮的花园和豪宅。虽然那天太阳火辣辣的,灰尘扑面,她们却非常快乐。要是用一个在文明的社会里常被忽略的词,她们就是"不顾一切地"偷摘枝条伸出篱笆的、秀色可餐的橙子。我没阻止她们,她们不知道那些灌木丛可以在熟练的花匠手中被弯成各种新奇的形状,所以,她们在旅行中不仅看到了美景,还觉得很新奇。我们还坐汽车去了波特查里恩湖。

你的弟弟
萨姆·克莱门斯
1860年3月
于圣·路易斯

22. Lincoln's Letter to Horace Greeley

这封信写于美国南北战争的关键时期,也是亚伯拉罕·林肯最著名的信件中的一封。格利里是极具影响力的《纽约论坛》主编,他写了一篇《二亿同胞的请愿书》向林肯政府缺乏明确的前进方向和决心提出了疑问并要求得到解答。林肯去世多年后,格利里为林肯写了一篇评论。他说,林肯总统不仅回答了自己的疑问,而且以此向美国人民表明了政府对解放黑奴的坚决立场。

Executive Mansion,
Washington, August 22, 1862

Dear Sir,

I have just read yours of the 19th addressed to myself through the New-York Tribune①. If there be in it any statements, or assumptions② of fact, which I may know to be erroneous③, I do not, now and here, controvert④ them. If there be in it any inferences which I may believe to be falsely drawn, I do not, now and here, argue against them. If there be perceptible⑤ in it an impatient and dictatorial⑥ tone, I waive⑦ it in deference⑧ to an old friend, whose heart I have always supposed to be right.

As to the policy I "seem to be pursuing" as you say, I have not meant to leave any one in doubt.

I would save the Union. I would save it

---

① New-York Tribune 《纽约论坛》
② assumptions [ə'sʌmpʃən] n. 假定,设想
③ erroneous [i'rəunjəs] adj. 错误的,不正确的
④ controvert [kɔntrə'və:t] v. 反驳
⑤ perceptible [pə'septəbl] adj. 可察觉的,显而易见的
⑥ dictatorial [ˌdiktə'tɔ:riəl] adj. 独裁的,独断专行的
⑦ waive [weiv] v. 放弃
⑧ deference ['defərəns] n. 顺从,尊重

the shortest way under the Constitution. The sooner the national authority can be restored; the nearer the Union will be "the Union as it was". If there be those who would not save the Union, unless they could at the same time save slavery, I do not agree with them. If there be those who would not save the Union unless they could at the same time destroy slavery, I do not agree with them. My paramount① object in this struggle is to save the Union, and is not either to save or to destroy slavery. If I could save the Union without freeing any slave I would do it, and if I could save it by freeing all the slaves I would do it; and if I could save it by freeing some and leaving others alone I would also do that. What I do about slavery and the colored race, I do because I believe it helps to save the Union; and what I forbear②, I forbear because I do not believe it would help to save the Union. I shall do less whenever I shall believe what I am doing hurts the cause, and I shall do more whenever I shall believe doing more will help the cause. I shall try to correct errors when shown to be errors; and I shall adopt new views so fast as they shall appear to be true views.

I have here stated my purpose according to my view of official duty; and I intend no modification③ of my oft-expressed personal wish that all men everywhere could be free.

Yours,
A. Lincoln

林肯致贺拉斯·格利里

亲爱的先生：

我已读过你那篇于本月19号在《纽约论坛》上署名给我的文章。如果文中有什么我认为是错误的声明或是对现实的假设，此时此刻，我不予以反驳；如果文中有什么我认为是错误的推论，此时此刻，我不会争辩。如果感

---

① paramount [ˈpærəmaunt] *adj.* 极为重要的
② forbear [fɔːˈbɛə] *v.* 忍耐，克制
③ modification [ˌmɔdifiˈkeiʃən] *n.* 更改，修改

觉文中有失去耐心和独断专行的口吻,我不会放在心上。我很尊敬这位老朋友,而且总是觉得他的想法是正确的。

对于你说的我"似乎正在实行的"政策,我没打算让任何人猜疑。

我会挽救这个合众国,我会依照宪法最快地挽救它。国家权威恢复得越早,那么合众国就会越快成为"过去的样子"。如果有人要奴隶制存在才愿意国家统一,我不会同意他们这样做;不废除奴隶制,就拯救不了这个合众国,不这样我就不赞同。这场斗争中我最高的目标就是拯救合众国,而不是挽救或废除奴隶制度。如果不释放一个奴隶就能够拯救国家,我愿意这样做;如果释放所有的奴隶能够拯救国家,我也愿意这样做;如果释放一些奴隶而不管剩下的奴隶可以拯救国家,我也愿意这样做。我之所以这样对待奴隶制和有色人种,是因为我相信这样会挽救整个国家;我之所以容忍我能容忍的是因为我不相信那样会挽救国家。无论何时我发现我所做的破坏了这个事业,我就不会继续做下去;当我发现我所做的有利于这个事业,我会再接再厉地做下去。当我犯了错误后,我将尽力改正;同样我会采纳新的观点,只要它们是正确的。

根据我对政府职责的看法,我在此申明我的观点;我不准备改变我经常表达的个人愿望:任何地方的任何人都是自由的。

此致

林肯

1986 年 8 月 22 日

于华盛顿行政大厦

23. Lincoln's Letter to George Robertson

乔治·罗伯逊律师是来自肯塔基州的国会议员、法律教授,曾经为林肯当过辩护律师。他送给过林肯一本关于奴隶制的小册子,为此林肯回复了以下信件。

August 15,1855

My Dear Sir,

　　The volume you left for me has been received. I am really grateful for the honor of your kind remembrance①, as well as for the book. The partial reading I have already given it, has afforded me much of both pleasure and instruction. It was new to me that the exact question which led to the Missouri compromise②, had arisen before it arose in regard to Missouri; and that you had taken so prominent③ a part in it. Your short, but able and patriotic speech upon that occasion, has not been improved upon since, by those holding the same views; and, with all the lights you then had, the views you took appear to me as very reasonable.

　　You are not a friend of slavery in the abstract. In that speech you spoke of "the peaceful extinction④ of slavery" and used other expressions indicating your belief that the thing was, at some time, to have an end. Since then we have had thirty six years of experience; and this experience has demonstrated⑤, I think, that there is no peaceful extinction of slavery in prospect for us. The signal failure of Henry Clay, and other good and great men, in 1849, to effect any thing in favor of gradual emancipation⑥ in Kentucky, together with a thousand other signs, extinguishes that hope utterly. On the question of liberty, as a

---

① remembrance [ri'membrəns] n. 回想,记忆,问候
② compromise ['kɔmprəmaiz] n. 妥协,折中
③ prominent ['prɔminənt] adj. 卓越的,显著的,突出的
④ extinction [iks'tiŋkʃən] n. 消失,消灭,废止
⑤ demonstrate ['demənstreit] vt. 示范,证明
⑥ emancipation [iˌmænsi'peiʃən] n. 释放,解放

principle, we are not what we have been. When we were the political slaves of King George, and wanted to be free, we called the maxim that "all men are created equal" a self evident truth; but now when we have grown fat, and have lost all dread of being slaves ourselves, we have become so greedy to be masters that we call the same maxim "a self evident lie". The fourth of July has not quite dwindled away;① it is still a great day—for burning fire-crackers!!!

That spirit which desired the peaceful extinction of slavery, has itself become extinct, with the occasion, and the men of the Revolution. Under the impulse of that occasion, nearly half the states adopted systems of emancipation at once; and it is a significant fact, that not a single state has done the like since. So far as peaceful, voluntary emancipation is concerned, the condition of the negro slave in America, scarcely less terrible to the contemplation② of a free mind, is now as fixed, and hopeless of change for the better, as that of the lost souls of the finally impenitent③. The Autocrat of all the Russias will resign④ his crown, and proclaim his subjects free republicans sooner than will our American masters voluntarily give up their slaves.

Our political problem now is "Can we, as a nation, continue together permanently⑤—forever—half slave, and half free?" The problem is too mighty for me. May God, in his mercy, superintend the solution.

Your much obliged friend, and humble servant

A. Lincoln

① dwindle away 减少,缩小
② contemplation [ˌkɔntemˈpleiʃən] n. 注视,沉思
③ impenitent [imˈpenitənt] adj. 不悔悟的,顽固的
④ resign [riˈzain] v. 辞去
⑤ permanently [ˈpəːmənəntli] adv. 永存地,不变地

林肯致乔治·罗伯逊

亲爱的先生：

您留给我的书已收到，非常感谢您亲切的问候，还有那本书。我已经阅读了其中一部分，从中感受到许多乐趣，并受益匪浅。直接导致密苏里州妥协的问题爆发在密苏里州问题出现之前，您在这个事件中起到了那么重要的作用，这些事情我都不知道。在那种情形下，您短小精悍却又有力的充满爱国精神的演讲没有被那些持同样观点的人做丝毫改动；而且，和您有着同样的态度，您的观点在我看来很有道理。

您不是一个只会空洞地谈论奴隶制的朋友。在那次演讲中您提到"和平终结奴隶制"，并且用其他方式表达了您的信念——在某个时候这件事终会结束。从那以后我们积累了36年的经验。我认为这些经验已经证明和平终结奴隶制是不可能的。1849年亨利·克利和其他善良伟大的先生们做了所有支持肯塔基州逐渐解放奴隶的事情，但最终还是失败了，这个信号和众多其他征兆一起使希望之火完全熄灭。就自由权而言，总的来说，我们并非是过去那样。当我们是英国国王乔治的政治奴隶并想获得自由的时候，我们喊出了"人人生而平等"这个显而易见的真理；但是如今当我们已变得强大，已经不用担忧自己会沦为奴隶时，却变得如此贪婪，想成为统治者，又把同一个格言说成"显而易见的谎言"。7月4日的意义并未减弱，它仍是个伟大的日子——放鞭炮的日子！

希望和平终结奴隶制的精神本身已经不复存在，那些革命者也是如此。在当时那种情形的驱动下，近一半的州都立即实行了解放政策；一个重要的事实是，从那以后并没有一个州这样做。关于和平自愿解放奴隶的问题，对于一个自由人来说，美国黑人奴隶的情形是很糟糕的；只要那些失去灵魂的奴隶主们不知悔改，这种情形绝没有变好的可能。哪怕俄国的君主辞去王位，宣告他的臣民会成为自由共和党人，我们美国奴隶主也不会主动放弃他们的奴隶。

我们目前的政治问题是"作为一个国家，我们能继续永久地让我们的民众一半是奴隶，一般是自由人，这样一起到永远吗？"这个问题对我来说太难了，请上帝施予仁慈，给出解决方案。

非常感激您的朋友与谦卑的仆人

林肯
1855年8月15日

24. Sullivan Ballou's Love Letter to His Wife

萨利文·巴罗和他27个亲密战友以及4000美国人牺牲在"第一个马纳萨斯"战役。在此之前一个星期,他给妻子写了这封信。

July the 14th, 1861

My very dear Sarah,

The indications are very strong that we shall move in a few days—perhaps tomorrow. Lest I should not be able to write you again, I feel impelled① to write lines that may fall under your eye when I shall be no more.

Our movement may be one of a few days' duration② and full of pleasure—and it may be one of severe conflict and death to me. Not my will, but thine God, be done. If it is necessary that I should fall on the battlefield for my country, I am ready. I have no misgivings about, or lack of confidence in, the cause in which I am engaged, and my courage does not halt or falter. I know how strongly American Civilization now leans upon the triumph③ of the Government, and how great a debt we owe to those who went before us through the blood and suffering of the Revolution. And I am willing—perfectly willing—to lay down all my joys in this life, to help maintain this Government, and to pay that debt.

But, my dear wife, when I know that with my own joys I lay down nearly all of yours, and replace them in this life with cares and sorrows—when, after having eaten for long years the bitter fruit of orphanage④ myself, I must offer it as their only sustenance⑤ to my dear little children—is it weak or dishonorable, while the banner of my purpose

---

① impelled [im'peld] adj. 迫不及待的
② duration [djuə'reiʃən] n. 持续时间
③ triumph ['traiəmf] n. 胜利
④ orphanage ['ɔ:fənidʒ] n. 孤儿身份
⑤ sustenance ['sʌstinəns] n. 食物,生计

floats calmly and proudly in the breeze, that my unbounded love for you, my darling wife and children, should struggle in fierce, though useless, contest with my love of country?

I cannot describe to you my feelings on this calm summer night, when two thousand men are sleeping around me, many of them enjoying the last, perhaps, before that of death—and I, suspicious that Death is creeping behind me with his fatal dart, am communing with God, my country, and thee.

I have sought most closely and diligently, and often in my breast, for a wrong motive in thus hazarding① the happiness of those I loved and I could not find one. A pure love of my country and of the principles have often advocated before the people and "the name of honor that I love more than I fear death" have called upon me, and I have obeyed.

Sarah, my love for you is deathless, it seems to bind me to you with mighty cables that nothing but Omnipotence② could break; and yet my love of Country comes over me like a strong wind and bears me irresistibly on with all these chains to the battlefield.

The memories of the blissful③ moments I have spent with you come creeping over me, and I feel most gratified④ to God and to you that I have enjoyed them so long. And hard it is for me to give them up and burn to ashes the hopes of future years, when God willing, we might still have lived and loved together and seen our sons grow up to honorable manhood around us. I have, I know, but few and small claims upon Divine Providence, but something whispers to me—perhaps it is the wafted prayer of my little Edgar—that I shall return to my loved ones unharmed. If I do

---

① hazard [ˈhæzəd] v. 冒险, 危险
② Omnipotence [ɔmˈnipətəns] n. 全能, 此处指"全能的上帝"
③ blissful [ˈblisful] adj. 有福的, 幸福的
④ gratify [ˈɡrætifai] v. 使满足

not, my dear Sarah, never forget how much I love you, and when my last breath escapes me on the battlefield, it will whisper your name.

Forgive my many faults, and the many pains I have caused you. How thoughtless and foolish I have oftentimes been! How gladly would I wash out with my tears every little spot upon your happiness, and struggle with all the misfortune of this world, to shield you and my children from harm. But I cannot. I must watch you from the spirit land and hover near you, while you buffet① the storms with your precious② little freight, and wait with sad patience till we meet to part no more.

But, O Sarah! If the dead can come back to this earth and flit unseen around those they loved, I shall always be near you; in the garish③ day and in the darkest night—amidst your happiest scenes and gloomiest hours—always, always; and if there be a soft breeze upon your cheek, it shall be my breath; or the cool air fans your throbbing temple④, it shall be my spirit passing by.

Sarah, do not mourn me dead; think I am gone and wait for thee, for we shall meet again.

As for my little boys, they will grow as I have done, and never know a father's love and care. Little Willie is too young to remember me long, and my blue-eyed Edgar will keep my frolics⑤ with him among the dimmest memories of his childhood. Sarah, I have unlimited confidence in your maternal care and your development of their characters. Tell my two mothers that I call God's blessing upon them. O Sarah, I wait for you there! Come to me, and lead thither my children.

Sullivan

---

① buffet [ˈbʌfit] v. 打击,搏斗
② precious [ˈpreʃəs] adj. 宝贵的,贵重的,珍爱的
③ garish [ˈɡæriʃ] adj. 炫耀的
④ throbbing temple 跳动的太阳穴
⑤ frolic [ˈfrɔlik] n. 嬉闹

萨利文·巴罗致妻子的情书

我最亲爱的莎拉:

强硬的命令已经下达,我们将要在几天之内出发,也可能就是明天。唯恐以后再不能给你写信,所以我迫不及待地为你写下这短短几行,万一我不在人世了,你将会看到它们。

我们的行军可能会持续一些时日,但将充满乐趣;对我来说,也可能会是一场严峻的冲突,死亡的临近。不是我的意志,而是你的上帝使然。如果我的国家需要我浴血沙场,我义无反顾。我对我所从事的事业毫无顾虑,亦不乏自信,我的勇气一往无前,坚定无比。我知道,美国文明目前迫切地需要依靠政府的胜利,我也知道,那些在我们前面饱受革命洗礼而倒在血雨腥风中的人们,我们亏欠他们太多。我情愿——绝对情愿——放弃此生所有的快乐以助维持政府稳定,并去偿还那一债务。

但是,我的爱妻,我知道,由于我个人的喜悦,我几乎剥夺了你所有的快乐,让你的生活充满牵挂和忧伤;当我长期饱受孤儿之苦,却必须要把它作为我挚爱的孩子们唯一的精神食粮——当我的决心之帜平静而自豪地飘扬于微风之中时,我对我挚爱的妻儿无边的爱却不得不无力地屈服于我对祖国之爱,这是软弱还是羞耻呢?

在这平静的夏夜我无法向你描述我的感情。此时两千战士正在我周围酣睡,他们中的许多人正享受着也许是他们死前最后的安静。我感觉到死神带着它那致命之剑正潜行于我背后,而我正在和上帝、我的祖国,还有你亲密对话呢。

我常在心中孜孜不倦地仔细寻找一个错误的动机,来危及我所爱的人的幸福,可始终没找到。对祖国和真理的无暇之爱得到人民的拥护,而"我所追求的荣誉之名超出我对死亡的恐惧"号召我,我唯有服从。

莎拉,我永远爱你,好比巨大的绳索把你我绑在一起,唯有全能的神才能将我们分离;然而,我对祖国的爱犹如一阵强劲的风将我义无反顾地推向战场。

与你共度过的幸福时光涌现在我的脑海,我对你和上帝充满感激和喜悦，我长久地享受着那些时光。让我将那些放弃并把对未来的希望付之一炬实属不易，如果上帝愿意，我们还要在一起生活、相爱并看着我们的儿子们在我们身边长大成人。我知道，我对神的眷顾几乎没有什么要求，但是仿佛有一些低声细语——也许是我的小埃德加的阵阵祈祷——告诉我我将安然无恙地回到我的亲人身边。如果我不能，我亲爱的莎拉，不要忘记，我是多么爱你，当我最后一缕气息消逝在战场上，它会窃窃私语你的名字。

请你谅解我许多的缺点，还有带给你的诸多痛苦。我曾经是多么的粗心和愚蠢！如果我能够用我的眼泪洗刷掉曾给你的幸福造成的污点，如果我能够和这个世界上的不幸作斗争以保护你和我的孩子们不受伤害，我该有多么高兴！但是我不能。当你以宝贵的、微弱的身躯搏击风雨，以悲恸的心情耐心等待我们相聚再不分离，我会在九泉之下关注你并会在你身边徘徊。

但是，莎拉！如果死去的人能够回到这个世界，并在他们所爱的人的周围悄然盘桓，我会守候在你的身边，在炫目的白天和漆黑的夜晚——在你幸福之中或忧郁之时——无时无刻；如果有微风拂过你的面颊，那将是我的呼吸；如果凉风吹拂你的鬓角，那将是我的灵魂掠过。

莎拉，不要哀悼我的死亡；只想像我只是离开并在等待着你，因为我们还要相见。

至于我的孩子们，他们将会像我一样成长，从来不知父亲的疼爱和关怀。小威利太小，不会对我有太深的记忆，蓝眼睛的小埃德加会在他童年最模糊的记忆中保留着我和他嬉戏的场景。莎拉，你充满母爱，会把他们培养成有品质的人，我对你有非常坚定的信心。告诉我的两个母亲，我会请求上帝保佑她们。莎拉啊，我会在那边等你！来我身边，带着我的孩子。

萨利文
1861 年 7 月 14 日

25. Lewis Carroll's Love Letter to Gertrude

刘易斯·卡洛尔(Lewis Carroll)的真名叫查尔斯·勒特威奇·道奇森(1832~1898),是一位数学家,长期在享有盛名的牛津大学任基督堂学院数学讲师,但他兴趣广泛,对小说、诗歌、逻辑都颇有造诣。使他成名的是《爱丽丝漫游奇境》(Alice in Wonderland)一书。

October 28, 1876

My Dearest Gertrude,

You will be sorry, and surprised, and puzzled, to hear what a queer① illness I have had ever since you went. I sent for the doctor, and said, "Give me some medicine. For I'm tired." He said, "Nonsense and stuff! You don't want medicine: go to bed!"

I said, "No; it isn't the sort of tiredness that wants bed. I'm tired in the face." He looked a little grave, and said, "Oh, it's your nose that's tired: a person often talks too much when he thinks he knows a great deal." I said, "No, it isn't the nose. Perhaps it's the hair." Then he looked rather grave, and said, "Now I understand: you've been playing too many hairs on the pianoforte②."

"No, indeed I haven't!" I said, "and it isn't exactly the hair: it's more about the nose and chin." Then he looked a good deal graver, and said, "Have you been walking much on your chin lately?" I said, "No." "Well!" he said, "it puzzles me very much. Do you think it's in the

---

① queer [kwiə] *adj.* 奇怪的,可疑的
② pianoforte [piˌɑːnəuˈfɔːti] *n.* 钢琴(piano 的旧称)

lips?" "Of course!" I said. "That's exactly what it is!"

Then he looked very grave indeed, and said, "I think you must have been giving too many kisses." "Well," I said, "I did give one kiss to a baby child, a little friend of mine."

"Think again," he said; "are you sure it was only one?" I thought again, and said, "Perhaps it was eleven times." Then the doctor said, "You must not give her any more till your lips are quite rested again." "But what am I to do?" I said, "because you see, I owe her a hundred and eighty-two more." Then he looked so grave that tears ran down his cheeks, and he said, "You may send them to her in a box."

Then I remembered a little box that I once bought at Dover, and thought I would someday give it to some little girl or other. So I have packed them all in it very carefully. Tell me if they come safe or if any are lost on the way.

Lewis Carroll

刘易斯·卡洛尔致格特鲁德的情书

我至爱的格特鲁德:

当你获知自从你走后我得了怎样一种怪病时,你将会感到难过、吃惊和困惑。我去看医生,说:"给我一些药吧,因为我很累。"他说:"胡说八道!你不需要药,睡觉去吧!"

我说:"不对。不是那种缺乏睡觉的疲劳。我脸部疲惫。"他看上去有点儿严肃,说:"噢,是你的鼻子累了。如果一个人认为自己知道很多,他总会滔滔不绝。"我说:"不。不是鼻子累。可能是头发。"他神情很凝重,说:"现在我明白了,你弹钢琴时太专注了。"

"不,事实上没有。"我说,"也不确定是头发,很有可能是鼻子和下巴。"他更严肃了,问:"你最近常闲扯吗?"我说:"没有。""那么,"他说,"这很让我迷惑不解。你认为是嘴唇里面累吗?""当然!"我说道,"正是!"

  他看起来真的严肃极了,说:"我想你一定是接吻太多了。""喔,"我说:"我确实吻过一个小宝贝一次,我的一个小伙伴。"

  "再想想,"他问,"你确信只有一次?"我又想了想,说:"可能是11次。"医生说:"你的嘴唇完全休息好之前不能再吻她了。""可是我怎么办呢?"我说,"你看啊,我还欠她182个吻呢。"他看上去心情很沉重,眼泪顺颊而流,说:"你可以放在一个盒子里寄给她。"

  我想起来我曾经在多佛买了一个小盒子并且想将来某一天把它送给某个小女孩。这不,我小心翼翼地将它们打包好了。告诉我它们是否安全抵达抑或在路途丢失。

刘易斯·卡洛尔
1876年10月28日

26. Robert Stevenson's Letter to Henry James

罗伯特·斯蒂文森(Robert Stevenson,1850~1894),苏格兰随笔作家、诗人、小说家、游记作家、新浪漫主义代表。斯蒂文森出生于苏格兰爱丁堡,早年就读于爱丁堡大学。他从学生时代起就酷爱文学,一生多病,但有旺盛的创作力。斯蒂文森的作品题材繁多,构思精巧,其探险小说和惊险小说更是富于独创性和戏剧性力量,其代表作《金银岛》、《化身博士》、《诱拐》等为他在读者中获得了巨大声望。

亨利·詹姆斯(Henry James,1843~1916),美国小说家、文学批评家、剧作家和散文家。他是19世纪美国现实主义文学的三大倡导者之一,他同豪威尔斯、马克·吐温一起,为美国现实主义文学的发展作出了积极贡献。他的《小说的艺术》(The Art of Fiction)一文所阐明的许多理论和观点,迄今依然被广泛地认为是无懈可击的经典之作。

以下是这两位作家就文学理论展开讨论的信。

December 8,1884

My dear Henry James,

This is a very brave hearing from more points than one. The first point is that there is a hope of a sequel①. For this I labored. Seriously, from the dearth② of information and thoughtful interest in the art of literature, those who try to practice it with any deliberate③ purpose run the risk of finding no fit audience. People suppose it is "the stuff" that interests them; they think, for instance, that the prodigious④ fine thoughts and

---

① sequel ['siːkwəl] n. 后续,随之而来的事
② dearth [dəːθ] n. 缺乏
③ deliberate [diˈlibəreit] adj. 深思熟虑的,故意的
④ prodigious [prəˈdidʒəs] adj. 巨大的

sentiments① in Shakespeare impress by their own weight, not understanding that the unpolished② diamond is but a stone. They think that striking situations, or good dialogue, are got by studying life; they will not rise to understand that they are prepared by deliberate artifice and set off by painful suppressions. Now, I want the whole thing well ventilated③, for my own education and the public's; and I beg you to look as quick as you can, to follow me up with every circumstance of defeat where we differ, and (to prevent the flouting④ of the laity⑤) to emphasize the points where we agree. I trust your paper will show me the way to a rejoinder⑥; and that rejoinder I shall hope to make with so much art as to woo or drive you from your threatened silence. I would not ask better than to pass my life in beating out this quarter of corn with such a seconder as yourself.

Point the second—I am rejoiced indeed to hear you speak so kindly of my work; rejoiced and surprised. I seem to myself a very rude, left-handed countryman; not fit to be read, far less complimented, by a man so accomplished, so adroit, so craftsmanlike as you. You will never have cause to understand the despair with which a writer like myself considers the park scene in Lady Barberina⑦. Every touch surprises me by its intangible⑧

① sentiment ['sentimənt] n. 情感
② unpolished [ˌʌn'pɔliʃt] adj. 未磨光的，无光泽的，未磨炼的
③ ventilate ['ventileit] v. 使通风
④ flout [flaut] v. 轻视，嘲笑
⑤ laity ['leiiti] n. 俗人，外行
⑥ rejoinder [ri'dʒɔində] n. 反驳
⑦ Lady Barberina 《芭博里娜夫人》，亨利·詹姆斯于1884年创作的一部长篇小说。
⑧ intangible [in'tændʒəbl] adj. 难以明了的，无形的

心灵的私语
Whisper of Soul: Letters from Famous People

precision; and the effect when done, as light as syllabub①, as distinct② as a picture, fills me with envy. Each man among us prefers his own aim, and I prefer mine; but when we come to speak of performance, I recognize myself, compared with you, to be a lout③ and slouch④ of the first water⑤.

Where we differ, both as to the design of stories and the delineation⑥ of character, I begin to lament. Of course, I am not so dull as to ask you to desert your walk; but could you not, in one novel, to oblige a sincere admirer, and to enrich his shelves with a beloved volume, could you not, and might you not, cast your characters in a mould a little more abstract and academic (dear Mrs. Pennyman had already, among your other work, a taste of what I mean), and pitch the incidents, I do not say in any stronger, but in a slightly more emphatic⑦ key—as it were an episode⑧ from one of the old novels of adventure? I fear you will not; and I suppose I must sighingly admit you to be right. And yet, when I see, as it were, a book of Tom Jones handled with your exquisite⑨ precision and shot through with those side-lights of reflection in which you excel, I relinquish⑩ the dear vision with regret. Think upon it.

---

① syllabub [ˈsiləbʌb] *n.* 奶油葡萄酒
② distinct [disˈtiŋkt] *adj.* 清楚的,明显的
③ lout [laut] *n.* 笨人
④ slouch [slautʃ] *v.* 懒散
⑤ of the first water 最上乘的,最好的
⑥ delineation [diˌliniˈeiʃən] *n.* 描绘
⑦ emphatic [imˈfætik] *adj.* 语势强的,用力的,显著的,断然的
⑧ episode [ˈepisəud] *n.* 插曲,插话,有趣的事件
⑨ exquisite [ˈekskwizit] *adj.* 优美的,高雅的
⑩ relinquish [riˈliŋkwiʃ] *v.* 放弃

As you know, I belong to that besotted① class of man, the invalid②: this puts me to a stand in the way of visits. But it is possible that some day you may feel that a day near the sea and among pinewoods would be a pleasant change from town. If so, please let us know; and my wife and I will be delighted to put you up, and give you what we can to eat and drink (I have a fair bottle of claret). —On the back of which, believe me, yours sincerely,

ROBERT LOUIS STEVENSON

罗伯特·斯蒂文森致亨利·詹姆斯

我亲爱的亨利·詹姆斯:

听从多家之言是一个勇敢的举动。第一个观点是要对未来充满希望。为此,我倍加努力。问题是由于在文学艺术中缺乏信息和富有思想的趣味性,那些心怀深思熟虑的目的的人努力实践,却找不到合适的观众。人们认为是素材使他们感兴趣,例如,他们认为莎士比亚作品中是惊人的思想和情感本身在给人以深刻的印象,却不理解未经打磨的钻石不过是块石头而已。他们认为动人的情节,或精彩的对白,是由研究生活得来的。他们不会更高层次地去理解这些是由熟练的技巧完成,并经痛苦挤压激发出来的。现在,为了我自己和公众的教育,我想把整件事情完全公开。我请求你尽可能快地阅读这封信,在我们意见不同的问题上跟我一起进行深入研究,并且(为了阻止门外汉的嘲笑)强调我们赞同的观点。我相信你的文章将会反驳我;并且你的反驳充满艺术性,让你想去追求,或者把你从恐惧的沉默中拯救出来。做你的援军一起弄清事情的真相,生活再没有比这更美妙的了。

第二,我真的很高兴能听到你高度评价我的工作,既欣喜又吃惊。对于我这样

---

① besotted [bi'sɔtid] *adj.* 愚蠢的,糊涂的
② invalid [in'vælid] *n.* 病人,残废者;*adj.* 有病的,残废的

一个粗鲁的、左撇子的乡巴佬作品,不适合像你这样如此才华横溢、如此熟练和懂得写作技巧的人去阅读,更不用提赞美了。你永远不会理解一个像我这样的作家在读《芭博里娜夫人》的公园场景时的绝望。我惊讶于每一个笔触的无形的精确性,它所达到的效果如奶油葡萄酒般清淡,如照片一样清晰,让我羡慕不已。我们中的每个人都更欣赏自己的目标,我也是这样;但当谈及表演时,我意识到和你相比,我是个头等的笨蛋和懒汉。

我们的分歧在故事的设计和角色的描绘方面,我开始悲叹。当然我还不至于愚蠢到让你放弃自己的风格的地步。但你能不能在一部小说中帮助一个真诚的倾慕者,用受欢迎的书卷丰富他的书架?你能不能,并且可不可以不把你的角色塑造得那么抽象和具有学术气息(亲爱的派尼曼夫人已经在你其他作品中体会到了我所提到的)?着重讲述事件,我不是说用再强些的音调,而是用稍微强调一些的音调——好比它是老式惊险小说中的一幕?我担心你不会,我想我必须叹息着承认你是对的。但是,当我看到它就像一本《汤姆·琼斯》,却被你用精确的手法处理和你所擅长的侧面描写来写,就遗憾地放弃了那甜蜜的幻想。请你想想吧。

正如你知道的,我是一个蠢人,一个病人,这让我不便于拜访。但是说不定你会感到在大海边和松树林中度过一天也是一个不错的选择。如果这样的话,请让我知道,我和我的妻子将会高兴地去接你,并且奉上我们所有的酒食(我有一大瓶红葡萄酒)。最后,相信我,你真挚的

罗伯特·路易斯·斯蒂文森
1884年12月8日

27. Pierre Curie's Love Letter to Mary

著名物理学家皮埃尔·居里(Pierre Curie,1859~1906)与妻子玛丽(Marie Curie,1867~1934)于1898年共同发现镭,于1903年共同获诺贝尔物理学奖。下面所选的信是皮埃尔写给玛丽的求爱信,开始时遭到了她的拒绝。但皮埃尔持之以恒的追求最终赢得了她的芳心,他俩于1895年结为夫妻。

August 10, 1894

Dear Marie,

Nothing could have given me greater pleasure than to get news of you. The prospect of remaining two months without hearing about you had been extremely disagreeable to me: that is to say, your little note was more than welcome.

I hope you are laying up a stock of good air① and that you will come back to us in October. As for me, I think I shall not go anywhere; I shall stay in the country, where I spend the whole day in front of my open window or in the garden.

We have promised each other—haven't we?—to be at least great friends. If you will only not change your mind! For there are no promises that are binding; such things cannot be ordered at will. It would be a fine thing, just the same, in which I hardly dare believe, to pass our lives near each other, hypnotized② by our dreams: your patriotic③ dream, our humanitarian④ dream, and our scientific dream.

Of all those dreams the last is, I believe, the only legitimate⑤ one. I mean by that that we are powerless to change the social order and, even

---

① to lay up a stock of good air 好好休息,注意身体
② hypnotize ['hipnətaiz] v. 施催眠术,使着迷
③ patriotic [ˌpætri'ɔtik] adj. 爱国的,有爱国心的
④ humanitarian [hju(ː)ˌmæni'tɛəriən] adj. 人道主义的,慈善的
⑤ legitimate [li'dʒitimit] adj. 合法的,合理的,正统的

if we were not, we should not know what to do; in taking action, no matter in what direction, we should never be sure of not doing more harm than good, by retarding① some inevitable evolution. From the scientific point of view, on the contrary, we may hope to do something; the ground is solider here, and any discovery that we may make, however small, will remain acquired knowledge.

See how it works out: it is agreed that we shall be great friends, but if you leave France in a year it would be an altogether too Platonic friendship②, that of two creatures who would never see each other again. Wouldn't it be better for you to stay with me? I know that this question angers you, and that you don't want to speak of it again—and then, too, I feel so thoroughly unworthy of you from every point of view.

I thought of asking your permission to meet you by chance in Fribourg. But you are staying there, unless I am mistaken, only one day, and on that day you will of course belong to our friends the Kovalskis.

Believe me your very devoted

Peirre Curie

皮埃尔·居里致玛丽的情书

亲爱的玛丽：

得到你的消息让我无比兴奋，一想到接下来两个月我将收不到你的来信，我又万分伤心。也就是说，你小小的便条让我十分快乐。

希望你保重身体，十月份回到我们这儿。至于我，我想我哪儿都不去，我只待在乡下，整日待在敞开的窗户前或花园中。

我们已经相互保证了，不是吗？至少做个很好的朋友，真希望你不会改变主意！因为我们的保证没有约束力，这种事情是不能随意作出命令

① retard [ri'tɑːd] v. 延迟，妨碍，阻碍
② Platonic friendship 柏拉图式的友谊，理想的但不切实际的友谊

的。我们彼此贴近度过余生,并用我们的梦想来催我们入睡:你的爱国之梦、我们的人道之梦以及科学之梦,这是件多么美好的事情,我几乎不敢相信。

在那些梦想之中,我想,只有最后一个是切合实际的。我的意思是我们无力改变社会秩序,就算我们有力,我们也不知从何做起。采取行动,无论朝哪个方向,我们都无法确信通过阻碍必然的发展是不是会带来好处,而不是更大的危害。相反,从科学的观点上讲,我们能够指望做些什么,科学的园地更为切实,因为我们所做的任何发现,无论多么小,都会成为已获的知识。

看看该怎么做:我们同意做个很好的朋友,但是如果一年后你离开法国,我们俩不再相见,那我们的友谊岂不成了柏拉图式的不切实际。你跟我待在一起难道不是更好些吗?我知道这个问题会让你生气,你不想重提;如果是那样,从任何角度看,我感到都配不上你。

我想请你允许我在弗里堡找机会与你见面。可是,如果我没弄错,你只在那儿待一天,而那一天你又属于我们的朋友柯伐斯基夫妇。

相信我是你真实的朋友

皮埃尔·居里
1894 年 8 月 10 日

28. Jack London's Love Letter to Anna Strunsky

杰克·伦敦(Jack London, 1876~1916),美国著名小说家。虽然家有妻室,他却爱上了同行安娜·斯特伦斯基(Anna Strunsky)。然而,杰克·伦敦声称自己不相信爱情,在下面的信中他就表露了这一思想。

Oakland, April 3, 1901

Dear Anna:

Did I say that the human might be filed in categories? Well, and if I did, let me qualify—not all humans. You elude me. I cannot place you, cannot grasp you. I may boast that of nine out of ten, under given circumstances, I can forecast their action; that of nine out of ten, by their word or action, I may feel the pulse of their hearts. But of the tenth I despair. It is beyond me. You are that tenth.

Were ever two souls, with dumb lips, more incongruously① matched! We may feel in common—surely, we ofttimes② do—and when we do not feel in common, yet do we understand; and yet we have no common tongue. We are unintelligible. God must laugh at the mummery③.

The one gleam of sanity④ through it all is that we are both large temperamentally⑤, large enough to often understand. True, we often understand but in vague glimmering ways, by dim perceptions, like

---

① incongruously [inˈkɔŋgruəsli] adv. 不调和地
② ofttimes [ˈɔfttaimz] 古英语 = often
③ mummery [ˈmʌməri] n. 哑剧表演,可笑的仪式
④ sanity [ˈsæniti] n. 心智健全
⑤ temperamentally [ˌtempərəˈmentli] adv. 气质地

ghosts, which, while we doubt, haunt① us with their truth. And still, I, for one, dare not believe; for you are that tenth which I may not forecast.

Am I unintelligible now? I do not know. I imagine so. I cannot find the common tongue.

Large temperamentally—that is it. It is the one thing that brings us at all in touch. We have flashed through us, you and I, each a bit of universal, and so we draw together. And yet we are so different.

I smile at you when you grow enthusiastic? It is a forgivable smile—nay, almost an envious smile. I have lived twenty-five years of repression②. I learned not to be enthusiastic. It is a hard lesson to forget. I begin to forget, but it is so little. At the best, before I die, I cannot hope to forget all or most. I can exult③, now that I am learning, in little things, in other things; but of my things, and secret things doubly mine, I cannot, I cannot. Do I make myself intelligible? Do you hear my voice? I fear not. There are poseurs④. I am the most successful of them all.

Jack

杰克·伦敦致安娜·斯特伦斯基的情书

亲爱的安娜：

我说过人可以入档归类吗？如果我说过，那就让我限定一下——不是所有的人。你就难倒了我，我无法将你归类，把握不住你。在特定情况下，我可以夸口到十之八九，我能预测到他们的行动。十个人中，我就可以通过他们的言语或行动感觉到九个人的心跳，但第十个总令我失望，我无法感知他们。你就是那第十个。

① haunt [hɔːnt] v. 神鬼出没
② repression [riˈpreʃən] n. 镇压，抑制，抑压
③ exult [iɡˈzʌlt] v. 狂喜，欢跃
④ poseur [pəuˈzəː] n. 装模作样的人，装腔作势的人

心灵的私语
Whisper of Soul: Letters from Famous People

两个嘴唇哑巴的人是很不相配的!我们可以有共同感受——当然,我们有时确实是那样——当我们没有共同感受的时候,我们反倒相互理解。然而,我们没有共同语言,不可理喻。上帝肯定会嘲笑我们的哑剧表演。

这整个过程中,有一丝理智的光芒,那就是我们俩都是性情中人,常常能相互理解。真的,我们经常相互理解,但是以模模糊糊的方式,隐隐约约地感知,像幽灵一样,它们在我们相互猜忌的时候常常用真实来光顾我们。仍然,我就是那一个不敢相信的人,因为你是我无法预感的第十个。

我现在不可理喻吗?我不知道,我想是这样的,我找不出共同语言。

性情中人——就是这样的。就是它让我们一直保持联系。我和你已一闪而过,每次都有一点儿共同之处,因而相互吸引,然而,我们俩太不同了。

当你热情高涨的时候,我在对你微笑吗?那是宽恕的微笑——不,那是接近嫉妒的微笑。25年来,我一直在压抑中生活,我学会了不热情,这是很难忘却的教训。我开始去忘记,但只是一点点儿。至少,在我死之前,我不能指望全部或大部分忘却。对于小事情,他人的事情,我可以欢呼雀跃,现在我正在学着这样做。但对于我自己的事情,尤其是秘密的事情,我无法欢呼起来,我无法。我能让自己变得可以理喻吗?你听见了我的声音吗?恐怕没有。世上有装模作样的人,我就是其中最成功的一个。

杰克
1901年4月3日于奥克兰

29. James Joyce's Love Letter to Nora Barnacle

詹姆斯·乔伊斯(James Joyce,1882~1941),爱尔兰作家,他创新的文学手法对现代小说有着深远的影响。《尤利西斯》(1922)是他创作的最为著名的意识流代表作。1904 年,他结识了诺拉·巴纳克尔(Nora Barnacle),在频繁的交往中,他们之间产生了爱情,并最终走到一起。

15 August,1904

My dear Nora,

It has just struck me. I came in at half past eleven. Since then I have been sitting in an easy chair like a fool. I could do nothing. I hear nothing but your voice. I am like a fool hearing you call me "Dear". I offended two men today by leaving them coolly. I wanted to hear your voice, not theirs.

When I am with you I leave aside my contemptuous①, suspicious nature. I wish I felt your head on my shoulder. I think I will go to bed.

I have been a half-hour writing this thing. Will you write something to me? I hope you will. How am I to sign myself? I won't sign anything at all,because I don't know what to sign myself.

James Joyce

---

① contemptuous [kən'temptjuəs] adj. 轻蔑的,侮辱的

詹姆斯·乔伊斯致诺拉·巴纳克尔的情书

我亲爱的诺拉:

我已经不知所措了。十一点半钟我就进来了,一直像个傻瓜似的坐在安乐椅子上,什么都做不了。耳朵里只听见你的声音。我像个傻瓜似的听着你叫我一声"亲爱的"。我今天得罪了两个人,因为我冷漠地离开了他们。我只想听听你的声音,而不是他们的。

跟你在一起时,我将轻蔑、怀疑的天性放在一边。我真希望能感受到你的头靠在我的肩膀上。我想我要上床睡觉了。

我花了半个小时写这点东西。你能给我写些什么吗?我希望你能。我怎样落款签名呢?我什么都不想签,因为我不知道我该签什么。

詹姆斯·乔伊斯
1904 年 8 月 15 日

30. Rupert Brooke's Love Letter to Noel

鲁佩特·布鲁克(Rupert Brooke,1887~1915),英国诗人,以写战争诗歌而闻名,其诗洋溢着浪漫的爱国精神。他死于第一次世界大战中。以下情书是他写给诺埃尔·奥利维尔的。

October 2,1911

Dear Noel,

I have a thousand images of you in an hour; all different and all coming back to the same... And we love. And we've got the most amazing secrets and understandings. Noel, whom I love, who is so beautiful and wonderful. I think of you eating omelet① on the ground. I think of you once against a skyline; and on the hill that Sunday morning.

And that night was wonderfulest of all. The light and the shadow and quietness and the rain and the wood. And you. You are so beautiful and wonderful that I daren't write to you... And kinder than God. Your arms and lips and hair and shoulders and voice—you.

Rupert Brooke

鲁佩特·布鲁克致诺埃尔的情书

亲爱的诺埃尔:

我一小时内回想起了你一千个图像,各不相同,然而到了脑海里就变成了一样……是的,我们相爱,我们分享了最奇妙的秘密和理解。我亲爱的诺埃尔,你是那么美丽,那么神奇。我想起你躺在地上吃着煎蛋卷,我想起你对着天际的样子:在那个星期天的早晨,在那座山上。

那一晚妙不可言,那光、那阴影、那静寂、那雨、那树林,还有你。你是那么美丽,那么神奇,我不敢将你描绘,你比上帝还仁慈。你的臂膀、你的双唇、你的头发、你的肩膀、你的声音以及整个的你。

鲁佩特·布鲁克
1911年10月2日

---

① omelet ['ɔmlit] n. 煎蛋卷

心灵的私语
Whisper of Soul: Letters from Famous People

31. Kafka's Love Letter to Felice

弗朗茨·卡夫卡一生中大部分时间是在一家保险公司当职员。他非同寻常的作品大部分都是在业余时间完成的，其中很多小说在他死于肺结核之后才发表。1912年，卡夫卡第一次邂逅菲莉斯·鲍威尔。5年后，他们上演的一场荡气回肠的情事最终以遗憾而收场。

11 November, 1912

Fräulein Felice,

I am now going to ask you a favor which sounds quite crazy, and which I should regard as such, were I the one to receive the letter. It is also the very greatest test that even the kindest person could be put to. Well, this is it:

Write to me only once a week, so that your letter arrives on Sunday—for I cannot endure your daily letters, I am incapable① of enduring them. For instance, I answer one of your letters, then lie in bed in apparent② calm, but my heart beats through my entire body  and is conscious only of you. I belong to you; there is really no other way of expressing it, and that is not strong enough. But for this very reason I don't want to know what you are wearing; it confuses me so much that I cannot deal with life; and that's why I don't want to know that you are fond of me. If I did, how could I, fool that I am, go on sitting in my office, or here at home, instead of leaping onto a train with my eyes shut and opening them only when I am with you? Oh, there is a sad, sad reason for not doing so. To make it short: My health is only just good enough for

---

① incapable [in'keipəbl] *adj.* 无能力的，不能的
② apparent [ə'pærənt] *adj.* 显然的，外观上的

myself alone, not good enough for marriage, let alone fatherhood. Yet when I read your letter, I feel I could overlook even what cannot possibly be overlooked.

  If only I had your answer now! And how horribly I torment you, and how I compel you, in the stillness of your room, to read this letter, as nasty a letter as has ever lain on your desk! Honestly, it strikes me sometimes that I prey like a spectre① on your felicitous② name! If only I had mailed Saturday's letter, in which I implored③ you never to write to me again, and in which I gave a similar promise. Oh God, what prevented me from sending that letter? All would be well. But is a peaceful solution possible now? Would it help if we wrote to each other only once a week? No, if my suffering could be cured by such means it would not be serious. And already I foresee that I shan't be able to endure even the Sunday letters. And so, to compensate④ for Saturday's lost opportunity, I ask you with what energy remains to me at the end of this letter: If we value our lives, let us abandon it all.

  Did I think of signing myself, Dein? No, nothing could be more false. No, I am forever fettered to myself, that's what I am, and that's what I must try to live with.

Franz

卡夫卡致菲莉斯的情书

菲莉斯小姐：

  我有一个请求，它听起来是如此疯狂；如果我是这封信的收信人，我也觉得疯狂，即使是最善良的人也会觉得这是最最严峻的考验。那么，这就是：

  每周只写一封信给我，这样你的信件就会在每周日到达——因为我无

---

① spectre [ˈspektə] n. 幽灵，妖怪
② felicitous [fiˈlisitəs] adj. 可喜的，善于措词的
③ implore [imˈplɔː] v. 恳求，哀求
④ compensate [ˈkɔmpənseit] v. 偿还，补偿，付报酬

心灵的私语

Whisper of Soul: Letters from Famous People

法忍受每天都有你的来信，我实在是不能够忍受它们。比如，我回复了一封你的信，然后躺在床上，表面上很平静，但我却心潮澎湃，满脑子里都是你。我属于你，实在是没有任何其他的方式来表达这种感情，全都没足够的表达力度。而正是因为这个原因，我并不想知道你现在是什么样的表情，它使我如此困惑，以至于我不能应付我的生活；这也是为什么我并不想知道你喜欢我。如果我知道，痴情的我怎会继续坐在办公室，或者待在家里，而不是闭着眼睛跳上火车，当只有我和你在一起的时候才睁开双眼？哦，有一个悲伤、很悲伤的原因让我不能够这么做。简单地说：我的健康状况让我只能够一个人孤零零地生活，不能结婚，更别说做父亲了。然而当我读到你的信时，我觉得我可以忽略任何一切不能够忽略的事情。

要是我现在就知道你的答复该多好！我是如此残酷地折磨你，强迫你在你的闺房里静静地阅读这封信，它是摆放在你书桌上的最令人讨厌的一封信！说实话，有时候我的脑海中会突然蹦出这么个念头：我像个幽灵一样蚕食了你快乐的名字！真希望我已寄出了星期六的那封信，在那封信中，我恳求你永远也不要再写信给我，并且我也作出了同样的承诺！上帝啊，是什么阻止了我寄出那封信？一切都会好的。不过现在还可能会有温和的解决办法吗？如果我们每星期只给彼此写一次信，会有用吗？不会的，要是我的痛苦能够用这样的办法医治，那么它就不是深深的痛苦了。而且我已经预见到了我甚至会无法忍受每周日的来信。所以，为了弥补周六失去的机会，在这封信末，我用我剩余的所有力量请求您：如果我们珍惜生命，那就让我们放弃这一切吧。

我想到署上我的名字了吗，戴恩？不，没有什么比这更虚假的了。不，我将永远被自己羁绊，这就是我，这就是我必须努力去忍受的。

弗朗茨
1912年11月11日

32. Bernard Shaw's Love Letter to Beatrice Campbell

乔治·萧伯纳(George Bernard Shaw,1856~1950),爱尔兰裔英国剧作家。作为费边社(Fabian Society)的一个创建者,他写了抨击社会的批评主义戏剧,包括《武器和人类》(Arms and the Man, 1894)、《茶花女》(Pygmalion,1913)及《圣女贞德》(Saint Joan,1923)。他曾获得1925年诺贝尔文学奖。

February 27,1913

To "Stella" Beatrice Campbell,
I want my rapscallionly① fellow vagabond②.
I want my dark lady. I want my angel—
I want my tempter.
I want my Freia with her apples.
I want the lighter of my seven lamps of beauty,honor,
laughter,music,love,life and immortality③... I want
my inspiration,my folly,my happiness,
my divinity,my madness,my selfishness,
my final sanity④ and sanctification⑤,
my transfiguration⑥,my purification⑦,
my light across the sea,
my palm across the desert,
my garden of lovely flowers,
my million nameless joys,
my day's wage,

---

① rapscallionly [ræp'skæljənli] adv. 像流氓地,无赖地
② vagabond ['væɡəbənd] n. 流浪者
③ immortality [imɔː'tæləti] n. 不朽
④ sanity ['sæniti] n. 心智健全
⑤ sanctification [ˌsæŋktifi'keiʃən] n. 神圣化,净化,圣洁
⑥ transfiguration [ˌtrænsfiɡju'reiʃən] n. 变形,变貌
⑦ purification [ˌpjuərifi'keiʃən] n. 净化

心灵的私语
Whisper of Soul: Letters from Famous People

my night's dream,
my darling and
my star…

George Bernard Shaw

萧伯纳致比阿特丽斯·坎贝尔的情书

致"斯特拉"比阿特丽斯·坎贝尔：
我需要我像恶棍一样的流浪伙伴。
我需要我的黑夫人，我需要我的天使——
我需要我的诱惑。
我需要我的拿着苹果的弗莱雅。
我需要点亮美丽、荣耀、欢笑、
音乐、爱情、生命和永恒七盏灯的打火机……我需要
我的灵感、我的愚昧、我的快乐、
我的神灵、我的疯狂、我的自私、
我最后健康的理智和圣洁、
我的转变、我的净化、
我的跨越海洋的阳光、
我的跨越沙漠的棕榈、
我的长着可爱鲜花的花园、
我许许多多的无名的欢乐、
我白天的薪水、
我晚上的梦、
我的知心爱人以及
我的星星。

乔治·萧伯纳
1913年2月27日

33. Woodrow Wilson's Love Letter to Edith Galt

伍德罗·威尔逊(Woodrow Wilson,1856~1924),美国第28届总统,曾获1919年诺贝尔和平奖。下面的情书是威尔逊总统写给伊迪丝·高尔特(Edith Galt)的,她后来成为威尔逊的第二任妻子。

The White House
September 19,1915

My noble, incomparable Edith,

I do not know how to express or analyze the conflicting emotions① that have surged like a storm through my heart all night long. I only know that first and foremost in all my thoughts has been the glorious confirmation you gave me last night—without effort, unconsciously, as of course—of all I have ever thought of your mind and heart. ②

You have the greatest soul, the noblest nature, the sweetest, most loving heart I have ever known, and my love, my reverence, my admiration for you, you have increased in one evening as I should have thought only a lifetime of intimate, loving association could have increased them.

You are more wonderful and lovely in my eyes than you ever were before; and my pride and joy and gratitude that you should love me with such a perfect love are beyond all expression, except in some great poem which I cannot write.

Your own,

Woodrow

---

① conflicting emotions 矛盾的情感,指"威尔逊原先不知道伊迪丝对他持何种感情,因而内心矛盾"。

② 此句结构复杂,应注意confirmation 和 of all I have ever thought of your mind and heart 之间的关系,它们被一系列的成分割裂开来。整句话的意思是:I only know that, in my mind, the most important thing has been that last night you gave me a positive answer to the suspicion that I laid on your mind and heart, and your confirmation made me very happy.

伍德罗·威尔逊致伊迪丝·高尔特的情书

我的高贵的、无与伦比的伊迪丝：

我不知道如何表达或分析这矛盾的情感，它如同暴风雨一般整晚在我心中汹涌澎湃。我只知道我头脑中首先想到的是你昨晚给我做出的、令我欣喜的肯定回答——毫不费力，情不自禁，理所当然——我一直想猜透你的想法和心事，而如今，你已令我释怀。

就我所知，你具有最伟大的心灵，最崇高的本性，最甜蜜、最可爱的内心。我本想一辈子的亲密和爱恋才会累积我的爱、我的敬意和爱慕，而你一晚上就让我增加了如此深的感情。

在我的眼中，你比以前更加可爱，更加奇妙。你爱我令我骄傲、令我欣慰，我对你充满感激，你完美的爱让我无法形容，只能用那些我写不出的诗来表达。

你的

伍德罗

1915 年 9 月 19 日于白宫

34. Katherine Mansfield's Love Letter to John Murry

凯瑟琳·曼斯菲尔德(Katherine Mansfield,1888~1923),新西兰出生的英国短篇小说作家。下面的情书是她写给约翰·穆里(John Murry)的,他们之间的爱情和婚姻持续了许多年,但突然间被凯瑟琳1923年因患肺结核去世而中断。

Saturday Night, May 19, 1917

My darling,

You are all about me—I seem to breathe you, hear you, feel you in me and of me.

What am I doing here? You are away. I have seen you in the train, at the station, driving up, sitting in the lamplight, talking, greeting people, washing your hands… And I am here—in your tent—sitting at your table.

There are some wall-flower petals on the table and a dead watch, a blue pencil and a Zeitung①. I am just as much at home as they.

When dusk came, flowing up the silent garden, lapping against the blind windows, my first and last terror started up. I was making some coffee in the kitchen. It was so violent, so dreadful I put down the coffee pot—and simply ran away—ran out of the studio and up the street with my bag under one arm and a block of writing paper and a pen under the other. I felt that if I could get here and find Mrs. F I should be "safe".

I found her and I lighted your gas, wound up your clock, drew your curtains and embraced your black overcoat before I sat down, frightened no longer. Do not be angry with me. That is why I am here.

When you came to tea this

---

① Zeitung 德语,"报纸"之意。

afternoon you took a brioche, broke it in half and padded the inside doughy bit with two fingers. You always do that with a bun or roll or a piece of bread. It is your way—your head a little on one side the while.

When you opened your suitcase, I saw your old Feltie and a French book all higgledy-piggledy①. "Tig②, I've only got 3 handkerchiefs." Why should that memory be so sweet to me?

Last night, there was a moment before you got into bed. You stood, quite naked, bending forward a little, talking. It was only for an instant. I saw you—I loved you so, loved your body with such tenderness. Ah, my dear!

And I am not thinking of "passion". No, of that other thing that makes me feel that every inch of you is so precious to me—your soft shoulders—your creamy warm skin, your ears cold like shells are cold—your long legs and your feet that I love to clasp with my feet.

It is partly because we are young that I feel this tenderness. I love your mouth. I could not bear that it should be touched even by a cold wind if I were the Lord.

We two, you know, have everything before us, and we shall do very great things. I have perfect faith in us, and so perfect is my love for you that I am, as it were, still, silent to my very soul.

I want nobody but you for my lover and my friend and to nobody but you shall I be faithful.

I am yours forever.

Tig

凯瑟琳·曼斯菲尔德致约翰·穆里的情书

亲爱的：

我的周围全是你——我似乎在呼吸你，倾听你，感觉你在我的身体里，感觉你属于我。

---

① higgledy-piggledy 重叠词，其意为"杂乱，紊乱"。
② Tig 媞格，是对 Katherine (凯瑟琳) 的昵称。

我在这儿做什么？你已离开，我看见你在火车里，在车站里，开着车，坐在灯光下，谈话，跟人打招呼，洗手……我在这里，在你的帐篷中，坐在你的桌子旁。

桌子上有些桂竹香的花瓣，还有一块不走的表，一支蓝色铅笔和一份报纸。我跟它们一样，就像在自家中。

黄昏临近时，风吹进寂静的花园，轻轻地拍打着百叶窗，我的第一个和最后一个恐惧开始了。我当时正在厨房煮咖啡。恐惧是那样的强烈，那样的可怕，于是我放下咖啡壶——只想跑开——跑出工作室，一只胳膊夹着包，另一只胳膊夹着一本书写纸和一支笔，跑到街上。我感到如果我能到达这儿，并找着F夫人，我才会"安全"。

我找着了她，然后点燃了你的煤气，将你的钟表上了发条，拉下窗帘，在我坐下之前，我拥抱了你黑色的大衣，然后不再感到害怕。请不要对我生气。这就是我来到这里的原因。

今天下午，你来喝茶的时候，你拿走了一块奶油糕点，将它掰成两半，并用两个指头捻着里面半熟的面包屑。你总是那样摆弄包子、卷子或面包。你就是那样——头微微偏向一边。

你打开手提包时，我看到了你的旧手帕和一本法语书，里面乱七八糟的。"媞格，我只带了三块手帕。"这些记忆对我来说为什么如此甜蜜？

昨天晚上，在你上床睡觉前有一会儿，你光着身子站着，身体微微向前倾斜地讲话。就在那一瞬间，我看见了你——我如此爱你，那样温柔地爱着你的身体，啊，我亲爱的！

我说的不是"激情"。不，而是其他的事情，让我感到你身体的每一寸都是那样的宝贵——你柔软的肩膀，你温暖滑润的皮肤，你的耳朵像贝壳一样凉爽——你修长的腿，你的脚，我多喜欢用我的脚将它们紧紧地夹住。

可能因为我们还年轻，我才感觉如此温柔。我喜爱你的嘴，如果我是上帝，我几乎不能容忍寒风会碰着你的嘴。

你知道在我们的面前，我们俩拥有一切，我们能够做出非常伟大的事情，我对我们完全充满信心，如同我对你的爱是那么完美，我的灵魂一如既往，默默无言。

我只要你做我的爱人和朋友，再没他人。我只忠诚于你。

我永远属于你！

媞格
1917年5月19日，星期六晚上

35. Helen Keller's Letters to Ter Teacher

海伦·凯勒(Helen Keller,1880~1968),是美国一位残障教育家。她在19个月大时因为一次猩红热而导致失明和失聪。后来在她的导师安妮·沙利文(Anne Sullivan)的努力下,她学会了说话,并开始和其他人沟通。她毕业于哈佛大学。以下两封信是她在老师外出度假期间写给老师的。

I

Montgomery, February 7, 1917

Dearest Teacher,

  We have just had the most terrible excitement; but, thank God, every one is safe and well. So don't be worried by the news in this letter.

  A fire broke out in my room Monday night. Fortunately I wasn't asleep. At first I noticed a strange odor①; but it was exactly like the odor of steam in the kitchen-pipe; so I paid no attention to it. Then came a light odor like smoke from out-of-doors. I had noticed it so frequently in our house and elsewhere, it didn't disturb me. But suddenly I smelt tar and burning wood. I sprang up, threw a window open and rushed to mother's room. She found a flame six feet high in my room and called Warren. Mildred telephoned to the fire-department②, and in an incredibly short time they arrived. I felt the men hacking away at the floor, we had gone down into Mildred's bedroom. A moment later we were all ordered out of the house. They said they couldn't tell where the fire would spread. So out we went bundled up in blankets and quilts, and went down the street to Grandma Tyson's. It was after one; we sat by the fire awhile and tried to calm down a little. Just as we were getting in bed, we got word that the fire was caused by a defective③ flue④. It had started right

---

① odor [ˈəudə] n. 气味,名声
② fire-department 消防队
③ defective [diˈfektiv] adj. 有缺陷的
④ flue [flu:] n. 烟洞,烟道,暖气管

under my bed! The firemen said that they had come just in time. Five or ten minutes more, and the house would have been demolished. ①

None of us got to sleep until four o'clock. We came home after breakfast. The firemen had made a great hole under my bed, and the chemicals which they used got on some of Mildred's furniture in the sitting-room. In the parlor② the smoke had been so dense that the wallpaper was black. But otherwise the house isn't badly damaged. We've lost nothing, the house is insured. But I suppose we shall be living with carpenters, painters and plumbers for a week or so. We're having trouble with the pipes too. It has been so cold—from nine to twenty above—that we've kept the water turned off; but two of the pipes burst last week.

I think Mildred had the only cool head in the family. She didn't try to put out the fire, she looked after the children and saw to it that we were all wrapped up. The fright affected mother more than any of us. She doesn't seem to be herself at all.

It distresses me to think that my lack of sight might have proved fatal to my loved ones. It seems as if I could never sleep quietly here again without putting my face down close to the floor and hunting all over for an odor or a hidden spark.

When are you coming back to America, Teacher? I hate to have you so far away while we're on the verge of war, and those dread submarines③ are scouring the ocean for whatever they can destroy.

The other night, when I returned from a call on Annie Keller, I found a telegram from the Enterprise Association asking for a short statement of my opinion of the plan to urge Congress to appropriate a hundred million dollars for the relief of non-combatants in all occupied territory. It

① demolished [di'mɔliʃ] v. 毁坏,破坏,推翻
② parlor ['pɑːlə] n. 客厅,会客室
③ submarine ['sʌbməriːn] n. 潜水艇,潜艇

was too late to reply, and I am not especially interested in that sort of philanthropy①. So I didn't bother about it. I suppose that would be a good thing for our government to do. We have criminally made millions upon millions out of the War, and ought to give back all we can.

I'll write later when there is more cheerful news. I don't want to tax your dear eyes. I enclose a sort of journal letter from Mrs. Thaw. How dear, brave and patient she is!

With love to Polly, and with the hope that she is keeping watch over your welfare like a Sherlock Holmes, I am

Your affectionate
Helen

II

Montgomery, March 16, 1917

Dearest Teacher,

I don't know when this letter will reach you, as the strike of the railroad brotherhoods has been called for tomorrow, and I am not sure that you will be here on the 14th of April. So I am taking this chance to tell you how I thank God at the remembrance of you on your birthday. Would it be as beautiful, as entirely joyous for you to remember as the day is for me when you gave birth to my mind! Yes, whatever the menace② of the years may be, my faith will speak. May the cruel tree of your sorrow put forth③ glowing blossoms of joy! May new strength and triumph wait upon you! May the sunshine of love still lie warm upon your brave life and you, my precious Teacher.

Polly's letter with the sweet message from the Porto Rico woods came Wednesday. It is uncanny④ how keenly I have felt all the delight and loveliness of your paradise, how I have adored it despite the unrest

---

① philanthropy [fɪˈlænθrəpi] n. 慈善事业
② menace [ˈmenəs] n. 威胁
③ put forth 提出
④ uncanny [ʌnˈkæni] adj. 离奇的

and anxiety about you that surrounded me, and how sad I feel now at the thought of your leaving it. It does not seem, as if I had been away from you all this weary① while; it seems as if I had dwelt with you in your wee camp, talked with you daily and touched your face many times a day in sheer gladness at your contentment②. This verse expresses my thought as really as if I had been there bodily.

"There is not in the wide world a valley so sweet

As that vale in whose bosom the bright water meet;

Oh! the last rays of feeling and life must depart

Ere the bloom of that valley shall fade from my heart.

Yet it was not that Nature had shed o'er the scene

Her purest of crystal and brightest of green;

'Twas not her soft magic of streamlet③ or hill—

Oh no! it was something more exquisite still.

'Twas that friends, the beloved of my bosom, were near,

Who made every dear scene of enchantment④ more dear."

I wish we could stay longer, until your soul was so rapt⑤ in the glory of our "joy isle" that your rough days of trial and heartache seemed as if they had never been! Perhaps in the face of all objections to an enervating⑥ climate that we hear, Porto Rico has done you a world of good, and it may be as well for you to remain until the heat of summer drives you away.

I don't want to leave the shack with all its adventures and gleeful associations either. But if we must, perhaps we can camp out in the Adirondacks or in Colorado.

① weary ['wiəri] *adj.* 疲倦的,厌倦的
② contentment [kən'tentmənt] *n.* 满意,知足
③ streamlet ['stri:mlit] *n.* 小溪,细流
④ enchantment [in'tʃɑ:ntmənt] *n.* 迷惑,着迷
⑤ rapt [ræpt] *adj.* 全神贯注的
⑥ enervate ['enə:veit] *v.* 削弱

Truly I want to shake myself out of this war and hear again the whispered messages from a happier world. Dreams are my only refuge from a life in which I have no part or lot.

I had a wonderful dream this morning. You and I stood, methought, on the ghastly battle-fields of Europe. The living were all retreating with a tumult① that stunned our senses. The dead lay piled around us—pillowed upon each other, and O my God, they were all young. One instant we gazed upon their marred, broken bodies, and our hearts seemed about to burst. Then they changed and the fury, the agony, the cruelties of war vanished. Angels were bending over those young forms and touching their foreheads. Beauty and light stole back into the marred faces, the shattered limbs became straight and whole, and the still hearts began to throb with revived joy. It was as if all the pain-throbs of the father-heart, all the tears of motherhood, all the warm kisses stored up in childhood's treasuries, all the pleadings of lonely young lives cast away②, all the deeds of love wrought faithfully unto the death had taken shape and stood around us, a shining host sanctifying that spot, that day. Under their pure hands the guns mouldered away, and the hates and wicked devices of all the warring powers fell at their feet ashamed. Vast multitudes of men and women gathered, fearless of cannon and death-raining steel towers, to minister to the young who had fallen and to those who were left mourning. Forgetting party, church, race, they raised a universal cry, "Cease slaying one another, we stand or fall here, now, we move not hence until you open the door of the poor hearts you have hunted and rekindle the home fires you have extinguished." It was a world of old people, women and babes pitted against a world of blood, naked valor of love against armed savagery! Rather than perish with their wives, mothers and little ones, the armies dispersed, enemies embraced weeping, and the battle-fields of Europe were again the world's precious granaries of life and joy.

---

① tumult [ˈtjuːmʌlt] *n.* 吵闹,骚动,拥挤
② cast away 抛弃

I have just been down for dinner. We spoke of the strike. It is worrying Mildred, as she may have to buy provisions① in advance. Of course I am with the railroad men; I wish the government would take over our industries. That seems the only logical thing to do.

Here is some pleasant news. You probably remember Miss Josephine Krisler, the girl with whom we drove in the Memphis suffrage② parade. Well, we read in yesterday's paper that she had succeeded in getting a bill passed to establish a commission③ for the blind of Tennessee. Isn't that fine? The south is waking up to the needs of its blind at last. That was a most interesting letter from Professor Walters. I shall answer it.

I enclose a pleasant letter which I have answered from a lady who heard us in Burlington, Vermont, and who visited Marjorie here this winter. I went walking with her several times, and her conversation was a joy to me, so interesting, so varied and full of enthusiasm④. We all wanted to know her better. She has traveled almost everywhere, and her mind is a rich storehouse of experience and sympathy. She is both charming and cultivated, quite a reformer, they say. As you will see from her letter, she is a great friend of Allan Benson.

What do you think happened to Warren sometime ago? He was out birdhunting. It was so misty he couldn't see very far. He thought once that he saw a bird a good way off and fired. Imagine his horror when the bird turned out to be a man throwing up his arms and shouting, "My God, I'm shot." Warren couldn't stir for a moment. But he found the man wasn't hurt at all.

I must stop now to mail this letter. With untold love to yourself, and with a hug for Polly, I am

Your affectionate
Helen

---

① provisions [prə'viʒəns] n. 供应,(一批)供应品
② suffrage ['sʌfridʒ] n. 投票,选举权
③ commission [kə'miʃən] n. 委任,委托
④ enthusiasm [in'θju:ziæzəm] n. 狂热,热心,积极性

海伦·凯勒致老师

其 一

最亲爱的老师:

  我们全家刚刚经历过一场最可怕、最惊心动魄的一幕。不过,谢天谢地,我们每个人都安然无恙,所以请不要再为我在信中的讲述而担忧。

  周一晚上,我的房间发生了一场火灾。庆幸的是,当时我并未熟睡。开始我闻到了一种奇怪的味道,就像是厨房排烟道里发出的气息,因此我没有在意。不久,从屋外飘来一股微微的烟雾气息。对于这种气息无论在家里还是在别处我都经常闻到,所以我仍不以为然。可是突然间我闻到一种焦油和燃烧的气息,我猛地跳了起来,打开一扇窗子,然后奔向母亲的房间。她发现我的房间烧起了足有六英尺高的火焰,就赶忙叫来渥伦。米尔德里德给消防队拨了电话,很快消防人员迅速赶到。我感觉到他们在地板上奋力地扑打着火苗,这时我们已转移到米尔德里德的卧室。过了一会儿,我们都被叫出了房间,消防员说他们也说不清火苗会蔓延到哪里,因此我们只好裹在毛毯和棉被里,沿着街道去泰森奶奶的家里避难。时间已过凌晨一点,我们在火炉旁坐了一会儿,心情稍稍平静。正当我们要上床休

息时,从消防员那里传来消息:火灾是由破损的烟道引起的,正好在我的床下起火。消防员说幸亏他们来得及时,如果再晚到 5 分钟或 10 分钟的话,房屋早就烧毁了。

  直到凌晨四点我们才重新入睡,早饭后我们回到家中。消防员们在我的床下凿了一个大洞,起居室里米尔德里德的家具上也沾上了一些消防用的化学喷剂。客厅里浓烟滚滚,壁纸都被熏黑了。但还好,房屋并没有受到很大的损坏,我们没有什么损失,因为房子上了保险。但我猜想这一周时间左右我们将整日与木匠、油漆工和水管工打交道了。我家的水管也出了问题:气温特低——华氏 9~20 多度,我们只好把水关掉了,但上周还是有两根管子被冻裂了。

  我觉得米尔德里德是家里唯一头脑冷静的人。她没有去试图扑灭火

焰,而是照看孩子们,负责把我们全部包裹得严严实实的。这场火灾对母亲影响特别大,她似乎和以前大不一样了。

想到我的双目失明可能会对我挚爱的家人造成致命的伤害,我忧心忡忡。从此以后,好像每晚如果我不把脸向下贴近地板,四处搜寻潜在的火星的气息,大概就再也不能安然入睡了。

老师,您何时回到美国?处在战争的边缘,那些可怕的潜水艇在海底四处巡逻,搜索可以击毁的目标,而我们却相隔如此遥远,这真是我所不愿看到的啊!

前几天,我拜访安妮·凯勒后回到家中,发现了一封公共事业协会发来的电报。要求我对于敦促国会拨款一亿美元用于被占国家非战人员的救济这一举动作出简短评论。现在回答这个问题已为时太晚,况且我本人对于这类慈善事业不感兴趣,因此我没有理会它。我想,对于我们的政府来说,这的确是一件善事。我们已从罪恶的战争中牟取无数暴利,现在该是我们返还的时候了。

有高兴的事情时我会再给您写信的,我不愿让您宝贵的眼睛过分受累。随信附上陶夫人日记体书信一封。您知道,她是多么亲切、勇敢而又耐心的一个人啊!

带去对波利的爱,希望她能随时监管好您的健康,就像福尔摩斯侦探一样。

您疼爱的
海伦
1917 年 2 月 7 日
于蒙哥马利

其　　二

最亲爱的老师:

我不知道这封信何时能到您的身边,因为铁路工人兄弟们已号召明天举行罢工,我不敢肯定 4 月 14 日您是否在这里。我只想借此机会告诉您,感谢上帝,让我在您生日这天想起了您。您是否也认为它是一个美丽、欢乐的日子呢,就像您赋予我的思想以生命的那天一样?是的,无论岁月如何残酷地流逝,我都会真诚地为您祈祷。我亲爱的老师,祝愿您的悲伤、冷峻之树开出灿烂的幸福之花!祝愿新的力量与胜利等待着您!祝愿爱的阳光洒满您勇敢的生活!

这周三我收到波利从波多黎各森林发来的一封信,信中带来甜蜜的问

候。在您那可爱的乐园里我感受到的无限快乐是难以言表的,即使对您的不安与焦虑始终围绕着我,我仍对它有着深深的眷恋。现在想到您要离开它,我的内心是多么伤感啊!仿佛在这段令人厌倦的时刻里,我并不曾离开您半步。相反,在您小小的野营地中我仿佛与您朝夕相处,谈天说地,当我一日数次地用手轻拂您的面庞时,您显得是那么心满意足。这首小诗真实地表达了我当时的思绪,仿佛我就身临其境:

"辽阔的世界里没有一条山谷如此甜蜜,
欢快流淌的小溪汇聚在它的怀抱里;
啊!山谷之花在我心中凋零之前,
生命和感情定会发出最后一缕光线。
然而大自然并没有在此美景上投射,
最为纯净的水晶和最为明亮的绿色;
那不是小溪和丘陵的温柔魔力——
啊,不!那是更为精致的东西。
那是朋友,我最深爱的人,越来越近,
她让每一片可爱景色更加美丽迷人。"

我希望我们能够长相厮守,直到您的心灵被我们"欢乐的岛屿"的光辉所环绕,直到您所经历的磨难和心痛一去不复返!或许就像在表面上讨厌我们所听说过的让精神萎靡不振的天气,然而波多黎各给您带来过不少益处。我建议您最好再待上一段时间,直到夏季逼人的暑气来临之前。

我真的不想离开棚屋,因为那里有那么多的惊险刺激和欢乐的聚会。但如果必须离开的话,我们可以到阿迪朗达克或是科罗拉多去露营。

我真想让自己从这场战争中摆脱出来,重新听到欢乐世界的喃喃低语,梦境是我不想介入现实生活的唯一避难所。

今晨我做了一个奇妙的梦。梦见你我二人,据我看来,站在恐怖的欧洲战场上,活着的人在一片混乱中撤退,让我们触目惊心。死去的人头枕着头,尸横遍野。哦,上帝呀!他们还那么年轻。凝视着这些受伤的、破碎的躯体,我们的心都要炸开了。忽然间,他们变了,战争的狂暴、痛苦与残酷消失得无影无踪。天使们俯下身来,用手轻轻抚摸年轻士兵们的前额。美丽与光彩又悄然回到那一张张破碎的面孔上,那些残肢断臂奇迹般地复员就位,完好无损,静止的心脏恢复了活力,发出欢快的跳动。似乎所有的父亲痛苦的心跳,母亲辛酸的泪水,珍藏在孩童时宝库里温暖的亲吻和孤独年轻生命的恳求全部都烟消云散了。爱的力量战胜死亡,来到人间。一大群人在神的护佑下显得熠熠生辉,神圣不可侵犯。枪支在他们圣洁的手中腐朽消融,怒火仇恨与邪恶的作战设备羞愧地瘫软在他们脚下。大批的男男女女聚集起来,面对大炮和枪林弹雨中的塔楼无所畏惧。他们搀扶起那些倒下的年轻身躯,并叫上那些留下为他们的战友哀悼的士兵。忘记了党派、宗教和种族,人们齐声呼喊:"停止相互残杀吧!我们同命运,共生死。我们会奋勇向前,直到你们敞开那可怜的心灵之门,并重新点燃你们那已经熄灭的生命之火。"这是一个由老人、妇女、孩子组成的世界与另一个嗜血成性的世界的对抗,这是完完全全的爱的勇气与荷枪实弹的野性之间的抗衡。士兵们没有向他们的妻子、母亲与孩子开枪,他们扔下武器,解散了部队,然后相拥而泣。欧洲战场再次变成人类生命与快乐的粮仓。

我刚刚下楼吃了晚餐,我们谈起了罢工。米尔德里德很是担忧,因为她得提前购买生活物资。当然我是站在铁路工人一方的,我希望政府能够接管工业。这才似乎符合逻辑。

这里有一则好消息。您也许还记得约瑟芬·克莱斯勒小姐吧,就是那个跟我们驱车一起去孟菲斯参加选举游行的那个女孩。从昨天的报纸上,我看到她使田纳西州建立盲人委员会的议案得以顺利通过。这不是一则好消息吗?南方终于觉醒,开始为盲人做些事情了,这也是沃尔特教授的来信中提到的趣事,我会给他回信的。

顺便附上一封令人愉快的信,这封信是一位夫人写给我的。她在佛蒙特州伯灵顿市时听说过我们,今年冬天还拜访了玛乔丽。我已回复了她的信件。我跟她散过几次步,跟她交谈真是一种乐趣:那么意趣盎然,内容丰富并激情四溢。我们都想跟她有更深的交往。她交游广阔,有着丰富的阅历和深深的同情心,她是一位有修养的、迷人的太太,并且是个改革家,他们都这么说。您从她的信中也可以看出,她是阿伦·本森的挚友。

您知道前段时间渥伦的事情吗?他出去猎鸟,但由于大雾,他看不清远方。有一次,他感觉看到不远处有一只鸟,于是就开枪射击。当那只鸟忽然间变成了一个人,举起双手叫道:"我的上帝啊,我被射中了"。您想像一下他有多惊恐:渥伦吓得一动也不敢动,可是最后他发现那人根本就没有受伤。

我得停笔去寄这封信了。带上对您无尽的爱,并拥抱波利。

您疼爱的
海伦
1917 年 3 月 16 日
于蒙哥马利

36. Eleanor Roosevelt's Letter to Helen Keller

艾琳娜·罗斯福(Eleanor Roosevelt,1884~1962)联合国外交家,人道主义者,富兰克林·罗斯福总统夫人,当时世界上最受人敬佩的妇女之一。她是西奥多·罗斯福的侄女,曾在英格兰求学。1905年与其远房堂兄富兰克林结婚。1945年罗斯福总统去世后,杜鲁门总统任命她为美国驻联合国代表,曾任联合国人权委员会主席。她对1948年世界人权宣言的起草和通过起了重要作用。

June 2, 1955

Dear Helen Keller,

It is a great pleasure to welcome you home and at the same time send you greetings on your 75th birthday.

From all sides I have been hearing of the wonderful job you have done on your goodwill① tour, and I have felt proud that you were representing our country. All of us when we go abroad are ambassadors② in our own right but I think your unselfishness

and deep devotion to the cause of humanity everywhere has a very special appeal. There can be no doubt that you left a spark of your spirit everywhere you went and that your efforts will produce good results for many years to come.

I feel sure that notes of praise and gratitude are pouring in to you but I think your greatest reward must lie in your own knowledge that you have left no stone unturned③ in trying to share your own inner happiness with all mankind.

---

① goodwill ['gud'wil] n. 善意,亲切
② ambassador [æm'bæsədə] n. 大使
③ left no stone unturned 把所有的石头都翻开,指"毫无保留地做……"

My affectionate greetings, and congratulations on a job well done. I hope you have a lovely birthday and that we will have the benefit of your inspiration① for many years to come.

Affectionately,
Eleanor Roosevelt

艾琳娜·罗斯福致海伦·凯勒

亲爱的海伦·凯勒:

  非常愉快欢迎您回国,并祝贺你75岁大寿。

  通过各种途径我一直听到您在亲善旅行中做得非常出色,并且我感到非常自豪您在代表着我们的国家。每个走出国门的人都是代表我们国家的大使,但您对人类事业的无私、博爱,使您的出行有着特别的吸引力。毫无疑问在您去过的地方都将留下您的精神的火花,您的努力在未来很多年都会有积极的影响。

  我确信表达人们赞美和感激的音符会涌向您,然而我认为您得到的最大奖励则是能毫无保留地和全人类分享您内心的幸福。

  这是我对一项伟大工作的赞美和祝贺。希望您度过一个愉快的生日,希望在未来许多年中我们会不断从您鼓舞人心的事业中受益。

仰慕您的
艾琳娜·罗斯福
1955年6月2日

---

① inspiration [ˌɪnspəˈreɪʃən] n. 灵感

37. Helen Keller's Letter to Eleanor Roosevelt

1942年至1952年之间,海伦·凯勒曾出访欧、亚、非、澳各大洲十三国,受到了各国的热烈欢迎。艾琳娜·罗斯福对其大加赞赏。在1955年凯勒75岁生日的那一天,她特地写信表示祝贺。在以下的信中,海伦·凯勒感谢罗斯福夫人的祝贺。

July 21, 1955

Dear Mrs. Roosevelt,

  Your telegram on my birthday sent a glow to my heart, and I should have thanked you long ago, but I have had an experience that you know well. A torrent① of work resulting from my world tour has swept me along, and I do not yet see any signs of terra firma②. However, I am proud that Polly and I were able to encircle③ the globe in the cause of the blind and the deaf, and that thought and your loving message and other wonderful remembrances made my natal day a beautiful memory that I shall cherish④ forever.

  With affection from Polly and myself, and with the prayer that you may long be spared in a world which still needs you, I am,

Lovingly your friend,
Helen Keller

---

① torrent ['tɔrənt] n. 急流,洪流
② terra firma [terə 'fəːmə] n. 陆地
③ encircle [in'səːkl] v. 绕……行一周
④ cherish ['tʃeriʃ] v. 珍爱,怀抱

海伦·凯勒致艾琳娜·罗斯福

亲爱的罗斯福夫人：

  您在我生日那天的来电温暖了我的心，我早就应该写信表达我的谢意，但您了解我的生活。世界之旅之后的工作洪流又将我卷入进去，到现在我还没看到任何要结束的迹象。但很庆幸因为聋哑我和波利能够环游世界，这种想法还有您的鼓励、赞美以及一些其他美好的记忆使我在我的生日里多了一份永远珍藏的回忆。

  向您致以波利和我的爱慕，在这个需要您的世界里，我会一直为您祈祷。

爱您的
海伦·凯勒
1955 年 7 月 21 日

38. Duff Cooper's Love Letter to Diana

达夫·库珀（Duff Cooper, 1890~1954），英国政治家兼外交家。1924年，他作为保守党成员被选入下议院。1931年8月，他被任命为财政大臣。1937年，他在丘吉尔内阁中担任情报部长。1945年，他从下议院退休之后担任英国驻法国大使。以下的信是他写给他未来的妻子黛安娜的。

August 20, 1918

Diana,

Darling, my darling. One line in haste to tell you that I love you more today than ever in my life before, that I never see beauty without thinking of you or scent happiness without thinking of you. You have fulfilled all my ambition, realized all my hopes, made all my dreams come true.

You have set a crown of roses on my youth and fortified me against the disaster of our days. Your courageous gaiety has inspired me with joy. Your tender faithfulness has been a rock of security and comfort. I have felt for you all kinds of love at once.

I have asked much of you and you have never failed me. You have intensified all colors, heightened all beauty, and deepened all delight. I love you more than life, my beauty, my wonder.

Duff Cooper

达夫·库珀致黛安娜的情书

黛安娜：

　　亲爱的，我的亲爱的。有一句话我急于想告诉你，我今天比这生中任何时候都更爱你，我看见了美就不得不想起你，感受到芳香的幸福也不得不想起你。你完成了我所有的抱负，实现了我所有的希望，使我所有的梦想成真。

　　你将玫瑰花冠戴在我年轻的头上，使我强有力地抵御岁月的灾难；你充满勇气的欢乐使我振奋起来；你温柔的忠诚成了我安全和舒适的磐石。我一下子感到了你各种各样的爱。

　　我要求你的太多，可你从不让我失望。你加强了所有的色彩，提高了所有的美丽，深化了所有的喜悦。我爱你超过了生命，我的美人，我的奇迹。

达夫·库珀
1918 年 8 月 20 日

39. Zelda Sayre's Love Letter to Fitzgerald

尽管我们对泽尔达·塞尔(Zelda Sayre)了解甚少,但弗朗西斯·斯科特·菲茨杰拉德(F. Scott Fitzgerald 1896~194)却是美国鼎鼎大名的作家,他是爵士时代的典型代表,他最著名的小说是《了不起的盖茨比》(The Great Gatsby,1925)和《夜色温柔》(Tender Is the Night,1934)。

Spring 1919

Sweetheart,

Please, please don't be so depressed—We'll be married soon, and then these lonesome nights will be over forever—and until we are, I am loving, loving every tiny minute of the day and night—

Maybe you won't understand this, but sometimes when I miss you most, it's hardest to write—and you always know when I calm myself—Just the ache of it all—and I can't tell you.

If we were together, you'd feel how strong it is—you're so sweet when you're melancholy①. I love your sad tenderness—when I've hurt you—That's one of the reasons I could never be sorry for our quarrels—and they bothered you so.

Scott—there's nothing in the entire world I want but you—and your precious love—All the material things are nothing.

I'd just hate to live a sordid②, colorless existence—because you'd soon love me less—and less—and I'd do anything—anything—to keep your heart for my own—I don't want to live—I want to love first, and live incidentally…

Don't—don't ever think of the things you can't give me—You've trusted me with the dearest heart of all—and it's so damn much more than anybody else in all the world has

---

① melancholy ['melənkəli] adj. 忧郁的,悲哀的
② sordid ['sɔːdid] adj. 肮脏的,污秽的

ever had—

How can you think deliberately of life without me—If you should die—O Darling—darling Scott—It'd be like going blind... I'd have no purpose in life—just a pretty—decoration.

I love you!

Zelda

泽尔达·塞尔致菲茨杰拉德的情书

亲爱的：

请你，请你不要如此沮丧，我们很快就结婚了，到那时，这样孤寂的夜晚就会永远结束，每一天，每一夜，每一分钟，我都会爱你，爱你，直到永远。

也许你不会理解这些。有时，我最想你的时刻却是我最难写作的时候——你总是明白我何时能使自己镇定——就凭这些痛苦——我不能向你倾诉。

如果我们在一起，你会感到它是多么的强烈——你的忧郁使你显得如此楚楚动人，我喜爱你忧伤的温柔——当我伤害你的时候——那就是我决不能原谅我们争吵的原因之一——争吵搅扰了你的安宁。

斯科特——在整个世界上，我别无所求，我只需要你——还有你宝贵的爱——所有物质的东西对我来说一文不值。

我讨厌污秽、没有色彩的生活——因为你对我的爱很快就会越来越少——越少——我得付出任何代价——任何代价——把你的心留住——我不需要生活——爱情是我的第一需要，生活只是附带的。

不要——千万不要想你不能给我的东西——你用最亲爱的心信任我——这大大地超过世界上的其他任何人能够做到的。

你怎能故意想象没有我的生活——如果你要死——啊，亲爱的——亲爱的斯科特——那就像世界变得黑暗——我的生命失去了意义——就像美丽的——装饰。

我爱你！

泽尔达
1919年春

40. Winston Churchill's Love Letter to Clemmie

温斯顿·丘吉尔(Winston Churchill, 1874~1965), 英国政治家、著作家, 1940~1945年, 1951~1955年两次任首相; 曾获1953年诺贝尔文学奖。下面的情书是他写给妻子克莱米(Clemmie)的。

January 23, 1935

My darling Clemmie,

　　In your letter from Madras① you wrote some words very dear to me, about my having enriched your life. I cannot tell you what pleasure this gave me, because I always feel so overwhelmingly in your debt, if there can be accounts in love…What it has been to me to live all these years in your heart and companionship no phrases can convey.

　　Time passes swiftly, but is it not joyous to see how great and growing is the treasure we have gathered together, amid the storms and stresses of so many eventful and to millions tragic and terrible years?

　　Your loving husband

Winston Churchill

---

　　① Madras 马德拉斯,印度东南部的一个城市,位于孟加拉湾的科罗曼德尔海岸。英国东印度公司于1639年在此建立圣·乔治要塞。马德拉斯从1746年到1748年被法国人占领。现在它是一个重要的工业、商业和文化中心,并有一个繁荣的港口(建于1862~1901年)。

温斯顿·丘吉尔致克莱米的情书

亲爱的克莱米:

　　你从马德拉斯寄来的信中写出的一些话语让我倍感亲切,你说到我让你的生活更加丰富。我无法告诉你这给了多么大的快乐,因为如果爱情有账户的话,我总是强烈地感到欠你的太多太多。任何词语也无法表达这些年来我是怎样活在你心中,与你相伴。

　　时间过得真快,然而,在这个多事之秋,在这个对于千百万人来说是那样悲惨可怕的年代里,在这样的暴风雨中和这样的压力下,我们还能难能可贵地相聚,想到这难道不令人欣慰吗?

　　爱你的丈夫

温斯顿·丘吉尔
1935 年 1 月 23 日

41. Winston Churchill's Letter to Franklin Roosevelt

1939年，第二次世界大战爆发，战争的硝烟也波及了英国，给英国人民带来了巨大的灾难，基本生活物资都很难得到保证。这时美国伸出了援助之手，给英国人民运去了大量的生活物资，从而确保了很多英国人渡过战争难关。时任英国首相的丘吉尔对此大为感动，特地给时任美国总统的罗斯福写信表示感谢。

June 14, 1942

MY DEAR MR. PRESIDENT,

  For a long time I have watched with grateful admiration the vast stream of gifts which from the first days of the War has been flowing from America to Great Britain for the relief of suffering and the succor① of distress, and in a volume which has barely lessened as a result of the advent of war to America, though a considerable diminution② of it was well to be expected. The generosity③ of these gifts, each one of which represents a personal sacrifice by an individual, is overwhelming and without precedent④. I am therefore anxious in the first place to express to you, Mr. President, the profound gratitude⑤ of the British people, and shall be glad if there is some way in which you may see fit to pass my feelings along to the American public.

  My second purpose in addressing you today is unhappily one of informing you that we now feel under the necessity of asking that this brotherly flow of material shall be diminished. It is not that the gifts are not

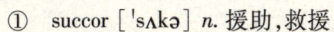

① succor ['sʌkə] n. 援助，救援
② diminution [ˌdimi'nju:ʃən] n. 减少，减低，缩小
③ generosity [ˌdʒenə'rɔsiti] n. 慷慨，宽大
④ precedent [pri'si:dənt] n. 先例
⑤ gratitude ['grætitju:d] n. 感激，谢意

desired—indeed they have constantly been ingeniously① devised to meet our real needs and the parcels from America have become a familiar and welcome feature in all the misfortunes which have overtaken our civilian population. The request which I am now compelled to make is due to additional demands on shipping resulting from the enormously increased flow of war materials for which ocean transport has to be provided. We shall have therefore to assign to goods of a more warlike character the shipping space which has hitherto② been available③ for the relief of our people—a sacrifice which we will make here without complaint, but not without very great regret.

As to the method of procedure, we have a Committee here—the American Gifts Committee—which hitherto has endeavored to ensure that gifts from America shall only be of a character that shall meet some real need. The Committee will now have to extend its activities and try to control the actual volume of gifts. A statement will shortly be issued to the press indicating the lines along which it is hoped to proceed.

I cannot conclude this letter, Mr. President, without affirming once again our gratitude for the comfort in days of suffering and of trial that was brought to us by the people of America, and our desire to make known our thanks.

Yours sincerely,
WINSTON S. CHURCHILL

---

① ingeniously [in'dʒiːnjəsli] adv. 有才能地,贤明地
② hitherto [ˌhiðə'tuː] adv. 迄今,至今
③ available [ə'veiləbl] adj. 可用到的,可利用的,有用的

温斯顿·丘吉尔致富兰克林·罗斯福

尊敬的总统先生：

很长时间以来，我注意到大批物资自战争开始就不断地从美国运往英国，从而减轻了我国人民的苦难和不幸，为此，我非常感激。由于战争波及美国，尽管预计救助会有大幅度的减少，但总量却几乎没有减少。这些礼物，每一份都代表着某个美国人的个人奉献，你们的慷慨是巨大的、史无前例的。首先，我迫切地想向您——总统先生——表达英国人民的感激之情，如果有某种您认为合适的途径来传达我对贵国人民的感激之情，我将会非常欣慰。

第二，我很遗憾地告诉您我们觉得您应该减少这种友好的物资援助，不是因为这些物资不是我们迫切渴望得到的。事实上这些物资在不断地满足我们真正的需要。在几乎夺去我们所有民众生命的灾难中，这些物资变成了为人熟知和讨人喜欢的东西。因为要运送的战争物资极大地增加，这些物资只能通过海运，因此我迫切地请求贵国给予额外的海上运输需求，我们不得不使战争物资来占据海上运输空间，这个空间一直都是用来为减轻我们人民的痛苦而服务的，我们要做出牺牲，虽然没有抱怨，但有遗憾。

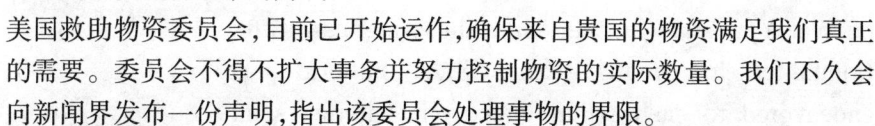

关于实施办法，我们成立了美国救助物资委员会，目前已开始运作，确保来自贵国的物资满足我们真正的需要。委员会不得不扩大事务并努力控制物资的实际数量。我们不久会向新闻界发布一份声明，指出该委员会处理事物的界限。

在遭受痛苦和考验的日子里，贵国人民给我们带来了安慰。在结束这封信之前，我再一次表达我们的感激之情，并希望让您和美国人民知道。

你的挚友

温斯顿·丘吉尔
1942年6月14日

42. Franklin Roosevelt's Letter to Winston Churchill

富兰克林·德拉诺·罗斯福(Franklin Delano Roosevelt, 1882~1945),美国第32位总统(1933年3月4日~1937年1月20日,1937年1月20日~1941年1月20日,1941年1月20日~1945年1月20日,1945年1月20日~1945年4月12日),是美国历史上唯一蝉联四届(第四届任期未满)的总统。罗斯福在20世纪的经济大萧条和第二次世界大战中扮演了重要的角色,被学者评为美国最伟大的三位总统之一。在下面的信中,他回复了丘吉尔1942年6月14日的信。

July 9, 1942

MY DEAR MR. PRIME MINISTER,

  I have received your letter of June 14, 1942 in which you express the gratitude of the British people for the vast stream of gifts which from the first days of the war has been flowing from America to Great Britain for the relief of suffering. You ask that this expression be conveyed to the American public.

  You say also that this flow of material must be diminished due to additional demands on shipping and that it will be necessary to assign to goods of a more warlike character the shipping space which has hitherto been available for the relief of the British people. You state further that the American Gifts Committee in Great Britain, which hitherto has endeavored to ensure that gifts from America shall meet some real need, will now try to control the actual volume of gifts.

  I am gratified by your statement that the relief sent from this country has given comfort to the British people during their days of great trial, and I shall give to the American people your expression of appreciation for the gifts they have provided. I am

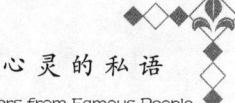

convinced that their action is indicative of the profound admiration felt in this country for the heroic stand of the British people against a barbarous① foe.

  You may be assured that we shall cooperate in every feasible② way with the American Gifts Committee in order to meet the situation brought about by the increased demand for shipping.

Very sincerely yours,
FRANKLIN D. ROOSEVELT

富兰克林·罗斯福致温斯顿·丘吉尔

尊敬的首相先生：

  我收到了您1942年6月14日的来信，信中您表达了英国人民感谢自战争开始之日起从美国源源不断运往英国的丰厚礼物，这些礼物使灾难得到了缓解。您要求一定要向美国民众传达您的这种感激之情。

  您也谈到由于对航运的更多需求和战备物资占据了更多的海上运输空间，本来这些空间是为运输救济英国人民的物资，所以现在这些物资一定要减少。您进一步强调英国的美国捐赠委员会确保这些救援物资满足人民的真正需要，现在他们正设法控制物资的实际数量。

  您说从美国运过去的物资在英国人民遇到灾难的时候给予了他们很大的帮助，还说我应该向美国人民转达您的感激之情，很感谢您的声明。我想他们是出于对英国民众对抗残酷敌人这个英雄壮举的敬慕之情。

  您放心，我们会与美国捐赠委员会以可行的方式合作，来满足不断扩大的航运需求。

您诚挚的
富兰克林·D. 罗斯福
1942年7月9日

---

① barbarous [ˈbɑːbərəs] adj. 野蛮的，残暴的
② feasible [ˈfiːzəbl] adj. 可行的，切实可行的

43. Franklin Roosevelt's Letter to Adolf Hitler

在1939年第二次世界大战爆发前夕，罗斯福给希特勒写了下面的这封信，他十分诚恳地劝告希特勒不要发动战争，并立即停止继续侵略他国，尽量以和平的政治协商来解决国际争端。然而，他的这封信并没有阻止第二次世界大战的全面爆发。

April 14, 1939

His Excellency Adolf Hitler, Chancellor of the German Reich,

    You realize, I am sure, that throughout the world hundreds of millions of human beings are living today in constant fear of a new war or even a series of wars.

    The existence of this fear—and the possibility of such a conflict—are of definite concern to the people of the United States for whom I speak, as they must also be to the peoples of the other nations of the entire Western Hemisphere. All of them know that any major war even if it were to be confined to other continents, must bear heavily on them during its continuance and also for generations to come.

    Because of the fact that after the acute tension in which the world has been living during the past few weeks there would seem to be at least a momentary① relaxation—because no troops are at this moment on the march—this may be an opportune② moment for me to send you this message.

    On a previous occasion I have addressed you in behalf of the settlement of political, economic, and social problems by peaceful methods and without resort to arms.

    But the tide of events seems to have reverted to the threat of arms. If such threats continue, it seems inevitable③ that much of the world must

---

① momentary [ˈməuməntəri] adj. 瞬间的，刹那间的
② opportune [ˈɔpətjuːn] adj. 凑巧的，恰好的
③ inevitable [inˈevitəbl] adj. 不可避免的，必然的

become involved in common ruin. All the world, victor nations, vanquished① nations, and neutral nations, will suffer. I refuse to believe that the world is, of necessity, such a prisoner of destiny. On the contrary, it is clear that the leaders of great nations have it in their power to liberate their peoples from the disaster that impends②. It is equally clear that in their own minds and in their own hearts the peoples themselves desire that their fears be ended.

It is, however, unfortunately necessary to take cognizance of③ recent facts.

Three nations in Europe and one in Africa have seen their independent existence terminated④. A vast territory in another independent Nation of the Far East has been occupied by a neighboring state. Reports, which we trust are not true, insist that further acts of aggression are contemplated⑤ against still other independent nations. Plainly the world is moving toward the moment when this situation must end in catastrophe⑥ unless a more rational way of guiding events is found. You have repeatedly asserted that you and the German people have no desire for war. If this is true there need be no war.

Nothing can persuade the peoples of the earth that any governing power has any right or need to inflict⑦ the consequences of war on its own or any other people save in the cause of self-evident home defense.

In making this statement we as Americans speak not through selfishness or fear or weakness. If we speak now it is with the voice of strength and with friendship for mankind. It is still clear to me that international problems can be solved at the council table.

It is therefore no answer to the plea for peaceful discussion for one

~~~~~~~~~~

① vanquished [ˈvæŋkwiʃt] adj. 被征服的
② impend [imˈpend] v. 进行威胁，即将发生
③ take cognizance of 认识到
④ terminate [ˈtɔːmineit] v. 停止，结束，终止
⑤ contemplate [ˈkɔntempleit] v. 凝视，沉思，预期，企图
⑥ catastrophe [kəˈtæstrəfi] n. 大灾难，大祸
⑦ inflict [inˈflikt] v. 造成，给予或强加给

side to plead that unless they receive assurances beforehand that the verdict① will be theirs, they will not lay aside their arms. In conference rooms, as in courts, it is necessary that both sides enter upon the discussion in good faith, assuming that substantial② justice will accrue③ to both; and it is customary and necessary that they leave their arms outside the room where they confer.

I am convinced that the cause of world peace would be greatly advanced if the nations of the world were to obtain a frank statement relating to the present and future policy of Governments.

Because the United States, as one of the Nations of the Western Hemisphere, is not involved in the immediate controversies④ which have arisen in Europe, I trust that you may be willing to make such a statement of policy to me as head of a Nation far removed from Europe in order that I, acting only with the responsibility and obligation of a friendly intermediary, may communicate such declaration to other nations now apprehensive⑤ as to the course which the policy of your Government may take.

Are you willing to give assurance that your armed forces will not attack or invade the territory or possessions of the following independent nations: Finland, Estonia, Latvia, Lithuania, Sweden, Norway, Denmark, The Netherlands, Belgium, Great Britain and Ireland, France, Portugal, Spain, Switzerland, Liechtenstein, Luxembourg, Poland, Hungary, Rumania, Yugoslavia, Russia, Bulgaria, Greece, Turkey, Iraq, the Arabias, Syria, Palestine, Egypt and Iran?

Such an assurance clearly must apply not only to the present day but

---

① verdict [ˈvəːdikt] n. 裁决,判决
② substantial [səbˈstænʃəl] adj. 坚固的,实质的
③ accrue [əˈkruː] v. 自然增加,产生
④ controversy [ˈkɔntrəvəːsi] n. 论争,辩论,论战
⑤ apprehensive [ˌæpriˈhensiv] adj. 有理解力的

also to a future sufficiently long to give every opportunity to work by peaceful methods for a more permanent① peace. I therefore suggest that you construe the word "future" to apply to a minimum period of assured non-aggression-ten years at the least—a quarter of a century, if we dare look that far ahead.

If such assurance is given by your Government, I shall immediately transmit it to the Governments of the nations I have named and I shall simultaneously② inquire whether, as I am reasonably sure, each of the nations enumerated③ will in turn give like assurance for transmission to you.

Reciprocal④ assurances such as I have outlined will bring to the world an immediate measure of relief.

I propose that if it is given, two essential problems shall promptly be discussed in the resulting peaceful surroundings, and in those discussions the Government of the United States will gladly take part.

The discussions which I have in mind relate to the most effective and immediate manner through which the peoples of the world can obtain progressive relief from the crushing burden of armament⑤ which is each day bringing them more closely to the brink of economic disaster. Simultaneously the Government of the United States would be prepared to take part in discussions looking toward the most practical manner of opening up avenues of international trade to the end that every Nation of the earth may be enabled to buy and sell on equal terms in the world market as well as to possess assurance of obtaining the materials and products of peaceful economic life.

At the same time, those Governments other than the United States which are directly interested could undertake such political discussions

---

① permanent [ˈpəːmənənt] adj. 永久的, 持久的
② simultaneously [siməlˈteiniəsli] adv. 同时
③ enumerated [iˈnjuːməreitid] v. 列举
④ reciprocal [riˈsiprəkəl] adj. 互惠的, 相应的
⑤ armament [ˈɑːməmənt] n. 军备, 武器

as they may consider necessary or desirable.

We recognize complex world problems which affect all humanity but we know that study and discussion of them must be held in an atmosphere of peace. Such an atmosphere of peace cannot exist if negotiations are overshadowed by the threat of force or by the fear of war.

I think you will not misunderstand the spirit of frankness in which I send you this message. Heads of great Governments in this hour are literally responsible for the fate of humanity in the coming years. They cannot fail to hear the prayers of their peoples to be protected from the foreseeable chaos① of war. History will hold them accountable for the lives and the happiness of all—even unto the least.

I hope that your answer will make it possible for humanity to lose fear and regain security for many years to come.

A similar message is being addressed to the Chief of the Italian Government.

FRANKLIN D. ROOSEVELT

富兰克林·罗斯福致阿道夫·希特勒

尊敬的德意志帝国总理阿道夫·希特勒阁下：

我相信,您一定意识到目前数百万世界人民生活在恐慌之中,他们害怕会爆发新的战争或是一系列的战事。

我代表美国人民想说的是,毫无疑问,美国人民最担心的就是唯恐发动战争和冲突,而这也是整个西半球其他国家和人民所关注的事情。所有人都知道,任何一次大规模的战争,即便是其他大陆的局部战争,也会在持续的过程中给他们甚至后世子孙带来严重的影响。

紧张的对峙之后,在过去的几周里,世界人民一如既往地生活着,看上去至少恢复了暂时的平静,因为此时没有军队在行进。正因为

---

① chaos [ˈkeiɔs] *n.* 混乱,混沌

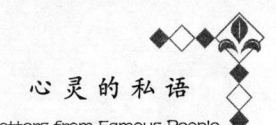

如此,我才有机会给您写这封信。

上一次,就以和平的方式解决政治、经济、社会问题,而不诉诸武力,我已和您交谈过。

但是事态的发展似乎又回到了武力威胁上。如果这样的威胁持续下去,那么世界大部分地方都会卷入毁灭之中,这种现象好像是不可避免的。全世界,无论是战胜国、战败国,还是中立国,都将遭此厄运。我不相信,全世界人民必将成为命运的囚徒。相反,很清楚的是大国的领导者有能力把人民从即将到来的灾难中解救出来。同样清楚的是,世界人民在他们的头脑中,在他们的心中都希望这种恐惧将会结束。

然而,不幸的是,我们必须认清最近发生的一些事实。

三个欧洲国家和一个非洲国家已经结束了他们的独立。远东另外一个独立国家的大部分领土已被邻国占领。报道坚称进一步的侵略行为会指向其他仍旧独立的国家,我们相信这些报道不是真的。简而言之,世界正走向毁灭,除非找到一种更加理性的方法来指导事态的发展。您反复强调您和德国人民不希望战争,如果这是真的,那就不需要战争。

除非在自我保卫战争中,否则谁都无法说服世界人民任何当权统治者有权利或需要将战争的后果强加给自己国家或其他国家。

这样陈述并不表明我们美国人自私、胆小、懦弱。我们是带着实力和友谊为人类呼吁请求的。在我看来,国家之间的问题显而易见应该在会议桌上来解决。

一方面要求和平谈判,一方面要求除非他们事先得到保证判决对他们有利,否则就不放下武器,对此,我们不予答应。在会议室里,就像在法庭上,双方有必要坦诚协商,假如双方得到公正实质的结果,那么把武器放在讨论协商的会议室外面,也就是很自然、很有必要的事情了。

我相信,如果世界各国能够得到贵国政府对目前及将来政策的坦诚声明,那么和平进程将会大大加快。

因为作为西半球的国家,美国并没有直接卷入欧洲发生的争端,我相信您会愿意给我这个远离欧洲国家的领导者一份政策声明。为此,带着责任与义务,我以一名友善的仲裁者的身份,与其他国家交流这一声明,他们会了解贵国政府做出决策的过程。

您愿意保证您的武装军队不会进攻或入侵以下独立国家的领土或附属地吗?它们是:芬兰、爱沙尼亚、拉脱维亚、立陶宛、瑞典、挪威、丹麦、荷兰、比利时、大不列颠及爱尔兰、法国、葡萄牙、西班牙、瑞士、列支敦士登、卢森堡、波兰、匈牙利、罗马尼亚、南斯拉夫、俄罗斯、保加利亚、希腊、土耳其、伊拉克、阿拉伯、叙利亚、巴勒斯坦、埃及和伊朗。

这样的承诺不仅适用于目前,而且要适用于遥远的未来,为了永久的和平,采取和平的手段来解决一切问题。因此,我建议,您要把未来这一概念理解为最低10年不侵犯——或25年,如果我们敢于看那么远的话。

如果您的政府做出这样的承诺,我会将此立即传达给我所提到的所有国家。并且,我会同时询问是否每个上面提到的国家都会向您做出同样的承诺,像我有理由相信的一样。

如果像我刚才规划的那样彼此承诺,那么世界冲突会立即得到缓和。

我建议,如果是这样,那么这两个基本问题应该立即在和平环境中进行讨论,而且美国政府会乐于参加这些讨论。

我认为,这些讨论要提到一些最有效的、最直接的方式,借此,世界人民可以从因沉重的军备负担而使他们日益接近经济灾难的情境中逐步得到缓解。同时,美国政府会做好参与讨论的准备,目的是开辟国际贸易最实际可行的方式,使地球上每个国家都能在世界市场公平的条例下买和卖,并且保证获得和平经济生活所需要的物质和商品。

与此同时,除美国政府以外,那些有兴趣的政府都可以参与一些他们认为是必要的或值得的政治讨论。

我们意识到复杂的世界问题影响着全人类,但是我们知道必须在和平的环境下研究、讨论这些问题。如果武力的威胁及战争的恐惧超过了协商的力量,那么和平环境将不会存在。

我想您不会误解我这么直言不讳地给您写这封信。此时此刻,大国政府的领导人对未来人类的命运负有不可推卸的责任。他们不能听不到人民祈求摆脱可预见的战争混乱,历史会证明他们是为所有生命和幸福负责的——即使是少数人的。

我希望阁下的回复能够让人类失去恐惧,为未来数年重获安全。

我也给意大利政府元首写了一封类似的信。

富兰克林·D.罗斯福
1939年4月14日

44. Franklin D. Roosevelt's Letter to the American Federation of Labor Convention

1941年10月,正当第二次世界大战如火如荼地进行的时候,美国劳工联盟举行了第61届年会。罗斯福总统通过《纽约时报》向大会致函以表祝贺。在信中,他还要求美国劳工全力以赴制造轮船、飞机、枪支、坦克等产品,支持世界人民的反法西斯战争。

October 8, 1941

New York Times,

Please extend my warm personal greetings to the officers and delegates attending the sixty-first annual① convention of the American Federation of Labor and my best wishes for a successful and constructive meeting in the interests of your members and all the American people. Your delegates represent the largest membership in the history of the federation.

This meeting is an event of international significance. It is a symbol of that freedom which we, in the United States, enjoy and must make every sacrifice to maintain.

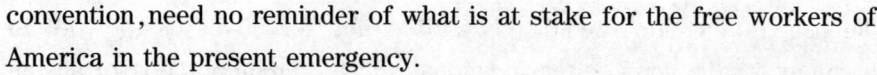

As hosts of distinguished② representatives of the underground labor movements of countries enslaved by Hitler, you, at this convention, need no reminder of what is at stake for the free workers of America in the present emergency.

The threat of Hitlerism is directed not only at labor, even though labor is among the very first that will suffer therefrom. It is aimed at all of us—every man, woman and child who believes in freedom. It menaces everything that we cherish as Americans and free men.

---

① annual [ˈænjuəl] adj. 一年一次的,每年的
② distinguished [disˈtiŋgwiʃt] adj. 卓著的,著名的,高贵的

The American people have, therefore, pledged everything in their power that those freedoms, without which free trade unions and free institutions cannot survive, shall never be taken away from them.

To protect those freedoms we shall, and must, devote every bit of human, physical and spiritual energy which we possess.

Our program of defense production of ships, planes, guns, tanks—must be all-out. It shall be limited by only one factor—the amount necessary to overwhelm the Nazi hordes①.

I know that every one of you, and the millions whom you represent, will lend every effort and make every necessary step to accomplish this end.

Every aspect of our national defense hinges on greater industrial production. The government has set up machinery to adjust industrial disputes in the full confidence that it is adequate② to solve problems which may arise on defense jobs in all fairness and justice to the parties concerned.

The Conciliation Service of the United States Department of Labor and the National Defense Mediation Board provide ample③ facilities for the adjustment of differences. The time has come when the services of such agencies must be used before any recourse is taken to a strike or lockout④, and I call now upon labor and management to cooperate at all times to that end.

This is not the time for idle promises. This is not the time to take chances with the national safety through any stoppage of defense work or defense production. Instead, this is the time for all of us to work in harmony for the good of the individual and the common good of all the people of these United States.

Every American owes that to himself and to the nation, which has

---

① horde [hɔːd] *n.* 一大群，一伙人
② adequate [ˈædikwit] *adj.* 适当的，足够的
③ ample [ˈæmpl] *adj.* 充足的，丰富的
④ lockout [ˈlɔkaut] *n.* 停工

given him so much.

Yes, this nation has given to you and given to me the right to life, liberty and the pursuit of happiness and these are among the greatest blessings of mankind. It is our job, our everlasting job, to preserve them as we have known them and to make whatever sacrifice is necessary as individuals or as groups in order to do so.

To do anything else would be to threaten their destruction and our own at the same time.

In this hour when civilization itself is in the balance, organizational rivalries and jurisdictional① conflicts should be discarded. Only by united action can we turn back the Nazi threat. The establishment of peace between labor organizations would be a patriotic② step forward of incalculable value in the creation of true national unity.

I am certain that the members of the American Federation of Labor will do their full part in carrying through the program to which we as a nation are committed and that all other responsible groups will do likewise. That is the contribution the American people will demand of③ all groups. That is the contribution the American people are determined they shall have for the preservation of home, family and nation.

Yours is a great responsibility. Workers in bondage throughout the world look to you as producers of the weapons of freedom to release them from slavery. I know you will not fail them.

FRANKLIN D. ROOSEVELT

① jurisdictional [ˌdʒuərisˈdikʃənl] adj. 司法的,司法权的
② patriotic [ˌpætriˈɔtik] adj. 爱国的,有爱国心的
③ demand of 要求

富兰克林·罗斯福致美国劳工联盟大会

《纽约时报》:

请将我个人的热情问候带给出席第61届美国劳工联盟大会的官员和代表们,预祝大会圆满成功,并能在大会所有成员和美国人民的利益问题上有建设性的成果。你们的代表是美国联盟历史上人数最多的群体。

这次大会是一个具有国际性意义的大事,它象征着我们在美国享受的并且必须做出牺牲去维持的那种自由。

作为在希特勒奴役下的各国地下劳工运动杰出代表的东道主,在这次大会上,我不需提醒你们在目前的紧急状况下什么在对美国自由工人造成威胁。

希特勒主义直接威胁的不仅仅是工人,虽然工人是第一批遭受威胁的人中的一部分。我们每个相信自由的男人、女人、孩子都受到了威胁;美国人和自由的人珍爱的任何事情都受到了威胁。

因此,美国人已经做出了保证,只要在他们的能力范围内,就没有人能剥夺自由贸易组织和自由机构的自由权利。

为了保护那些自由,我们应该而且必须将我们所拥有的每一点儿物质和精神上的力量都贡献出来。

我们要全力以赴制造轮船、飞机、枪支、坦克等产品,只有当这些产品的数量已经足够战胜纳粹党一伙人时才会限制生产。

我知道你们每一个人和你们代表的成千上万的人将付出一切所需要的努力来完成这个最终目标。

我们国防任何方面都围绕大工业生产旋转,政府已经建立起协调工业纠纷的机构,并充分相信它有能力公平公正地解决国防工作中所出现的问题。

美国劳工部门和国防调停理事会的调解机构会为各种各样的调解提供足够的设备。在对罢工或停工采取任何措施之前,这些调解机构要发挥作用,我要号召工人和经营者为完成那个目标而合作到底,这样的时刻已经到了。

现在不是空洞许诺的时候,不是通过中止防卫工作或者停止生产来威胁国家安全的时候,相反,这是我们所有人为了个人和所有美国人的利益而融洽地在一起合作的时候。

每个美国人都应该为了自己,为了让他受益很多的国家而做这些事情。

是的,国家已经给予你和我生存、自由和追求幸福的权利,这些都是上帝对人类最大的恩惠;当我们了解了这些,无论是个人还是团体都要不惜任何代价来维护它们,这是我们的职责,永远的职责。

而做其他任何事情都会威胁它们的毁灭,同时也威胁到我们自己的毁灭。

当前,人类文明前途未卜,我们应该抛弃组织内部的斗争和管辖权的冲突,只有通过联合行动才能抵抗纳粹的威胁,劳工组织之间建立和平是在真正的国家团结中向前迈进了不可估量的、爱国的一步。

我确信美国劳工联盟的成员们将会尽最大努力把这项事业进行到底,这是我们整个民族都不懈追求的,而且其他任何有责任感的团体也会这样做。这是美国人民要求所有团体要作的贡献,是美国人民决定为保护家园、家庭和国家所作的贡献。

你们有着强烈的责任感,全世界受压迫的工人把你们看作为自由而生产武器并把他们从奴役中解放出来的缔造者。我知道你们是不会让他们失望的。

富兰克林·D. 罗斯福
1941 年 10 月 8 日

45. Harry Truman's Letter to Kupcinet

  1945 年 8 月,历时 6 年多,使几千万人失去生命的第二次世界大战终于结束了。尽管全世界都在庆祝战争的结束,但关于是否是原子弹的使用带来战争结束的问题依然有着激烈的争论。"我认识到原子弹的悲剧意义,"在日本政府投降之前,哈里·杜鲁门总统在一家电台曾说过,"但我们是为了缩短战争带给人们极度的悲痛才使用的,是为了拯救成千上万人的生命和成千上万的美国青年。" 18 年后,杜鲁门对这件事的态度依然强硬,为此他一直遭到批判。他很感激那些曾经支持过他的人。1963 年 7 月,芝加哥《太阳时报》的艾文·库普辛那写了一篇称赞杜鲁门和赞同他的决策的专题文章,杜鲁门写下了下面这封信作为回复。

August 5, 1963

Dear Kup,

  I appreciated most highly your column of July 30th, a copy of which you sent me.

  I have been rather careful not to comment on the articles that have been written on the dropping of the bomb for the simple reason that the dropping of the bomb was completely and thoroughly explained in my Memoirs, and it was done to save 125,000 youngsters on the American side and 125,000 on the Japanese side from getting killed and that is what it did. It probably also saved a half million youngsters on both sides from being maimed① for life.

  You must always remember that people forget, as you said in your column, that the bombing of Pearl Harbor was done while we were at peace with Japan and trying our best to negotiate② a treaty with them.

  All you have to do is to go out and stand on the keel of the Battleship in Pearl Harbor with the 3,000 youngsters underneath it who had no

① maim [meim] v. 使残废
② negotiate [ni'gəuʃieit] v. 商议,谈判

chance whatever of saving their lives. That is true of two or three other battleships that were sunk in Pearl Harbor. Altogether, there were between 3,000 and 6,000 youngsters killed at that time without any declaration of war. It was plain murder.

I knew what I was doing when I stopped the war that would have killed a half a million youngsters on both sides if those bombs had not been dropped. I have no regrets and, under the same circumstances, I would do it again—and this letter is not confidential①.

Sincerely yours,
Harry S. Truman

哈里·杜鲁门致库普辛那

亲爱的库普：

非常感谢您给我寄来 6 月 30 号那篇专栏文章。我一直很小心地不去评论那些写关于投放原子弹的文章，这个原因我已经在我的回忆录里完全而且彻底地作过解释，原子弹的投放是为了挽救 12.5 万美国青年和 12.5 万日本青年不被杀害，结果也确实是这样，而且它还可能避免了双方 50 万青年成为终身残废。

您一定一直记得人们所忘记的东西。正如您在专栏里写的，"珍珠港事件"是发生在我们与日本处于和平的时期，当时我们还在尽力与他们拟订一份条约。

您一定要站在珍珠港里的"战斗号"战舰的甲板上，3000 年轻的生命就在下面，他们当时根本没有挽回生命的机会。沉没在珍珠港里的另外两三艘战舰也遭遇了同样的厄运，总共有 3000 到 6000 年轻的生命在当时没有宣战的情况下被杀害。那是赤裸裸的谋杀。

当我制止了那场如果原子弹没有投放就会使双方 50 万年轻人被杀害的战争时，我知道我在做什么，我从没有后悔过。如果出现同样的情况，我还会这样做。——这封信不属于机密。

您忠诚的
哈里·S. 杜鲁门
1963 年 8 月 5 日

---

① confidential [ˌkɔnfiˈdenʃəl] adj. 秘密的，机密的

46. President Kennedy's Letter to Governor Vandiver

约翰·肯尼迪(John Kennedy,1917~1963),美国第 35 任总统,他的任期从 1961 年 1 月 20 日开始到 1963 年 11 月 22 日在达拉斯遇刺身亡为止。他是在美国颇具影响力的肯尼迪政治家族的一员,被视为美国自由主义的代表。在第二次世界大战期间,他曾在南太平洋英勇救助了落水海军船员,因而获颁紫心勋章。肯尼迪在 1946~1960 年期间曾先后任众议员和参议员,并于 1960 年当选为美国总统,成为美国历史上唯一信奉罗马天主教的总统。

October 26,1960

Dear Governor,

  The nation and the world are watching Atlanta and its handling of the current① sit-in problem. I was pleased to learn on Monday that the principals on both sides have responded to civic and government leadership and have begun negotiations under amiable② conditions. I am confident that Atlanta's long tradition of good race relations will insure a peaceable and just settlement of this problem.

  However, I am surprised and disturbed with reports that as a result of his being a demonstrator Reverend Martin Luther King is being directed by a State Court in DeKalb to serve four months in a prison work camp under a suspended sentence for violating an automobile registration statute.③ I feel sure that under Georgia justice punishment in a prison work camp is meted out only to those whose offenses are major and largely involve crimes of moral turpitude④. It seems hard to argue that violation of an automobile registration statute involves moral turpitude. I have great respect for the people of Georgia and for their

---

 ① current ['kʌrənt] *adj.* 当前的,通用的
 ② amiable ['eimjəbl] *adj.* 亲切的,和蔼可亲的
 ③ statute ['stætjuːt] *n.* 法令,条例
 ④ turpitude ['təːpitjuːd] *n.* 奸恶,卑鄙

desire and sense of justice. I am sure that a cornerstone① of Georgia justice is that the punishment should fit the crime. Hence, I cannot believe that it is the public will that such a severe punishment be meted out for what is almost universally considered a technical violation punishable at most with a small fine. I neither desire nor seek to interfere② in the administration of Georgia justice, but as a friend of the people of Georgia and as an American citizen I do wish to inform you of my interest.

With best personal regards, I am

Sincerely,
John F. Kennedy

肯尼迪总统致范迪佛州长

亲爱的州长：

　　全国和全世界都在关注亚特兰大及其对目前静坐问题的处理。我很高兴地获悉双方主要领导人在周一已经回应了市民和政府的领导，并在友好的气氛下开始协商问题。我深信亚特兰大良好种族关系的悠久传统将确保和平公正地解决这一问题。

　　然而，有令我吃惊和不安的报道说，由于示威游行，马丁·路德·金牧师被德考勃州法院控告，并被判在监狱工作营地服刑4个月，缓期执行，罪名是违反汽车登记规定。我确定根据佐治亚司法处罚条例，在监狱营地的工作只分配给那些罪行重大或者罪行涉及道德沦丧的人；然而似乎很难说违反汽车登记规定是涉及道德沦丧的行为。我非常尊重佐治亚人民和他们的意愿以及正义感，我深信，佐治亚法律的基石是惩罚与罪行相符。因此，我不相信如此重的处罚是出于公众的意愿。众所周知这仅仅是一个技术性犯规，最多给予较少的罚款。我既不渴望，也无意干预佐治亚州政府的公正司法，但作为佐治亚人民的朋友，作为一个美国公民，我想告诉您我的意思。

　　致以个人的敬意

诚挚的

约翰·F. 肯尼迪
1960年10月26日

① cornerstone [ˈkɔːnəstəʊn] n. 墙角石，基础
② interfere [ˌɪntəˈfɪə] v. 干涉，干预，妨碍，打扰

47. Ronald Reagan's Love Letter to Nancy

罗纳德·里根(Ronald Reagan),生于1911年,美国第四十任总统(1981~1989年)。他原是一个演员,后成为政治活动家,1967~1975年任加利福尼亚州州长;在1980年的总统大选中,他击败了当时的在职总统吉米·卡特。他的政策特点是使经济复苏,对格林纳达、中美洲、黎巴嫩和利比亚进行军事干预,改善与苏联的关系。

Aboard Air Force One
March 4 1983

Dear First Lady,

  I know tradition has it that on this morning, I place cards—Happy Anniversary cards—on your breakfast tray. But things are somewhat mixed up. I substituted① a gift & delivered it a few weeks ago.

  Still this is the day, the day that marks 31 years of such happiness as comes to few men. I told you once that it was like an adolescent's② dream of what marriage should be like. That hasn't changed.

  You know I love the ranch but these last two days made it plain I only love it when you are there. Come to think of it that's true of every place & every time. When you aren't there I'm no place, just lost in time & space.

  I more than love you, I'm not whole without you. You are life itself to me. When you are gone I'm waiting for you to return so I can start living again.

  Happy Anniversary & thank you for 31 wonderful years.

  I love you!

Your Grateful Husband

---

① substitute [ˈsʌbstitjuːt] v. 用人或事来取代
② adolescent [ˌædəuˈlesnt] n. 青少年

罗纳德·里根致南希的情书

亲爱的第一夫人：

我知道我今天早晨要坚持传统，我要将贺卡——周年纪念贺卡——放在你的早餐盘里面。但是事情有时会弄混，几个星期前，我用礼物替代贺卡寄出去了。

今天就是很少有人能享受到的幸福 31 年纪念。我曾经对你说过婚姻像什么，就像青少年的梦。那仍然没有改变。

你知道我喜欢那个牧场，但就在这两天我才明白只有你在那儿我才喜欢它。想一想，其实，我在任何地点和时间的感受都是这样。只要你不在，我哪儿都不是，迷失在时空之中。

我十分爱你，没有你我就不完整。你是我的生命。你走了之后，我就等着你回来，以便于我能重新开始生活。

周年快乐，并感谢你给了我 31 年的美妙时光！

爱你

你充满感激的丈夫

1983 年 3 月 4 日

在空军一号上

48. Ronald Reagan's Letter to the American People

1994年,美国前总统里根被诊断患有阿尔茨海默氏老年性痴呆病,这种病让人失去短暂性的记忆,认知能力退化,并导致病人生活不能自理。为了唤起公众对身体健康的重视,里根夫妇决定写信公开自己的病情,并感谢美国人民对他的关心。

Nov. 5 1994

My Fellow Americans,

　　I have recently been told that I am one of the Americans who will be afflicted① with Alzheimer's Disease②.

　　Upon learning this news, Nancy & I had to decide whether as private citizens we would keep this a private matter or whether we would make this news known in a public way.

　　In the past Nancy suffered from breast cancer and I had my cancer surgeries. We found through our open disclosures we were able to raise public awareness③. We were happy that as a result many more people underwent testing. They were treated in early stages and able to return to normal, healthy lives.

　　So now, we feel it is important to share it with you. In opening our hearts, we hope this might promote greater awareness of this condition. Perhaps it will encourage a clearer understanding of the individuals and families who are affected by it.

　　At the moment I feel just fine. I intend to live

---

　　① afflict [ə'flikt] v. 使痛苦,折磨
　　② Alzheimer's Disease 一种老年性痴呆病,多发生于中年或老年的早期,因德国医生阿尔茨海默(Alois Alzheimer)最先描述而得名。症状是短期记忆丧失,认知能力退化,逐渐变得呆傻,甚至生活完全不能自理。
　　③ awareness [ə'wεənis] n. 知道,晓得

the remainder of the years God gives me on this earth doing the things I have always done. I will continue to share life's journey with my beloved Nancy and my family. I plan to enjoy the great outdoors and stay in touch with my friends and supporters.

Unfortunately, as Alzheimer's Disease progresses, the family often bears a heavy burden. I only wish there was some way I could spare Nancy from this painful experience. When the time comes I am confident that with your help she will face it with faith and courage.

In closing let me thank you, the American people for giving me the great honor of allowing me to serve as your President. When the Lord calls me home, whenever that may be I will face it with the greatest love for this country of ours and eternal optimism for its future.

I now begin the journey that will lead me into the sunset of my life. I know that for America there will always be a bright dawn ahead.

Thank you, my friends. May God always bless you.

Sincerely,

Ronald Reagan

罗纳德·里根致美国人民

我的美国同胞：

我最近得知我也成了一名受老年痴呆症折磨的美国人。

得知这个消息，南希和我不得不决定作为普通公民我们是要将一件私事保密还是公之于众。

过去，南希曾患有乳腺癌，我也做过治疗癌症的手术。我认为我们公开事实可以提高公众的意识。我们很高兴因此有越来越多的人去接受检查，他们接受早期的治疗而且完全康复，又过着正常健康的生活。

所以现在，我们认为与你们一起分享是很重要的，坦诚地说，我们希望这将能更好地提高人民对健康状况的意识。或许这将会鼓励那些受疾病影响的个人或家庭对此有一个更清晰的理解。

目前我感觉还好，我打算用上帝给我的在这个地球上剩下的日子做我一直做的事，我要继续与我深爱的南希和家人共享生命之旅。我计划要尽情享受户外活动，和我的朋友和支持者们保持联系。

但不幸的是,随着老年痴呆症的进一步加重,家人经常忍受着沉重的负担,我只是希望有办法可以让我减轻南希的这段痛苦的经历。当那一天到来时,我相信在你们的帮助下她会有信心和勇气去面对。

最后,我要感谢美国人民,是你们给了我这个莫大的荣幸,让我作为你们的总统为你们服务。无论何时上帝召我回去,我都会以我对这个国家最深的爱和对它的未来永远乐观地去面对它。

现在我即将步入人生暮年的旅程,我知道美国会有一个光明的未来。

谢谢你们,我的朋友们。愿上帝永远保佑你们。

你们真诚的
罗纳德·里根
1994 年 11 月 5 日

49. Tom Watson's Letter of Resignation

2006年9月,由于英国首相布莱尔的政策受到了许多英国人的攻击,他的内阁里就有七位高级官员提出辞呈,包括时任英国国防大臣的汤姆·华森。以下就是华森向布莱尔递交的辞职信。

Wednesday September 6 2006

Dear Tony,

The Labor Party has been my life since I was 15 years old. I have served the Party at every conceivable level and your own leadership since 1994 in a dozen different capacities, latterly as MP for West Bromwich East, a Government Whip①, and as Parliamentary Under-Secretary of State at the Ministry of Defense. My loyalty② to you personally, as well as to the Party and the values we stand for, has been absolute and unswerving③. The struggle to fashion the kind of credible, convincing, effective Labor Party you now lead has been the preoccupation of my adult years.

My pride in what our government has achieved under your leadership is beyond expression. We have revolutionized the lives and expectations of millions of our citizens, combining social justice with prosperity④ in a way which is unprecedented in the history of our country. Your leadership has been visionary and remarkable. The party and the nation owes you an incalculable debt.

So it is with the greatest sadness that I have to say that I no longer believe that your remaining in office is in the interest of either

---

① Whip [(h)wip] n. 党鞭,相当于党的总书记
② loyalty ['lɔiəlti] n. 忠诚,忠心
③ unswerving [ʌn'swə:viŋ] adj. 不偏离的,坚定的,始终不渝的
④ prosperity [prɔs'periti] n. 繁荣

the party or the country. How and why this situation has arisen no longer matters. I share the view of the overwhelming majority of the party and the country that the only way the Party and the Government can renew itself in office is urgently to renew its leadership.

For the sake of the legacy you have long said is the only one that matters—a renewed Labor party re-elected at the next general election—I urge you to reconsider your determination to remain in office.

As you know, I had a conversation with the Chief Whip last night, in which she asked me to withdraw my support from the 2001 intake's letter calling on you to stand down, or my position would be untenable① as a government minister. I have reflected on this overnight. I cannot withdraw my name, and therefore I accept her judgment.

I do not believe that statements so far give us the clarity necessary to progress over the next year. Nor do I believe that newspaper reports of potential dates which may have appeared since I signed the 2001 intake's letter can provide the clarity the party and the country so desperately need.

It is with the greatest regret, therefore, that I must leave the Government.

Yours ever,
Tom Watson

汤姆·华森的辞职信

亲爱的托尼：

自从我15岁以来，工党就成了我的命根子，我在你能想象的每个层面上为工党服务。自从1994年以来，我在许多种不同的职位上为您的政府效力，最近担任过威斯特·布龙维奇东区下议院议员、政府党鞭和驻国防部议会副部长。我忠于您个人、忠于工党以及我们所代表的价值观，这一点是绝对的和坚定不移的。我的成年时光一直在全心全意地努力将您领导的工党打造成可靠、可信、有效率的政党。

---

① untenable [ʌnˈtenəbl] adj. 防守不住的，不能维持的

我对我们政府在您的领导下所取得的成就有着无法表达的自豪感。我们已经彻底改变了千百万公民的生活和期望值,并在我国历史上史无前例地将社会公正与繁荣结合起来。您的领导才能一直都很卓越非凡,工党以及整个国家都从中受益无穷。

所以,我怀着最大的痛苦不得不对您说,我不再认为您继续执政符合党和国家的利益。这一情况是如何产生以及为何产生已不再重要。我和工党以及整个国家的绝大多数人都认为工党和现任政府继续执政的唯一道路就是紧急更换领导。

您一直在说唯一至关重要的事情就是在下一次大选中重新选举更新过了的工党,为此,我强烈要求您重新考虑您继续执政的决心。

正如您知道的那样,昨晚,我和首席党鞭举行了会谈,她请我撤出对2001年计划纳入信的支持,这封信要求您暂时辞退,不然的话,我作为政府大臣的职位就保不住。我通宵思考了这一问题,我不能撤出我的名字,所以,我接受她的裁决。

我不认为那些话到目前为止能明确地给我们指出了进入下个年度的道路。自从我在计划纳入信上签字以来,报纸上就有可能已经安排好对选举日期的报道,我也不认为这些新闻报道能够提供党和国家急需的明确性。

所以,非常非常遗憾,我要离开政府了。

永远忠于您的
汤姆·华森
2006年9月6日星期三

50. Tony Blair's Letter to Tom Watson

对于国防大臣汤姆·华森的辞职,布莱尔感到很痛心,他称赞了华森出色的工作,感谢他为政府所作的贡献。在以下信中,布莱尔解释了工党的政治路线,要结束以往的对立分裂。

Wednesday September 6, 2006

Dear Tom,

Thank you for your letter. I am sorry it has come to this. You did a good job as a minister and I thank you for it.

I know you have worked hard for the Labor Party throughout your life. I also accept entirely that you are entitled to① your view about the best way for the Labor Party to renew in office.

But as you will know from the long years of opposition we have endured, Labor only came to power after putting behind it the divisive behavior of the past and uniting around a modern vision for both country and party.

The way to renew and win again now is not to engage in a divisive—and since I have already made it clear I will be leaving before the election—totally unnecessary attempt to unseat the party leader, less than 15 months after our historic third term victory; but through  setting out the policy agenda for the future combined with a stable and orderly transition② that leaves ample time for the next leader to bed in.

We are three years from the next election. We have a strong policy platform. There is no fundamental③ ideological divide in the Labor Party

---

① be entitled to 有……的资格
② transition [trænˈziʒən] n. 转变,转换
③ fundamental [ˌfʌndəˈmentl] adj. 基础的,基本的

for the first time in 100 years of history. For the first time ever, we have the prospect① not just of two but three successive full terms.

To put all this at risk in this way is simply not a sensible, mature or intelligent way of conducting ourselves if we want to remain a governing party.

So I am sorry we are in disagreement.

Yours ever,
Tony

托尼·布莱尔致汤姆·华森

亲爱的汤姆:

感谢你的来信！事情发展成这样我很难过。你作为大臣，工作干得很好，我也谢谢你做的一切。

我知道你毕生都在为工党努力奋斗，而且我完全接受你有权利对工党重新执政的最佳方式发表意见。

但是你也知道我们忍受多年来的对立分裂。要想执政，就得抛弃过去的分裂行为，围绕为国为党的新观点联合起来。

重新执政并且再一次获胜的道路不是要通向分裂，因为我已经声明将在大选之前辞职，在我们取得历史性第三次执政期还不到 15 个月之时，完全没有必要去尝试罢免党的领袖，但是通过制定未来政策计划和一个稳定有序的过渡期，为下一任领导上任留有充裕的时间。

到下次大选还有 3 年时间。我们有强大的政策平台。工党在近 100 年的历史中第一次有基本意识形态上的分歧。第一次，我们期望不仅仅有两个而是三个连续圆满的执政期。

但是，即使我们想继续成为执政党，但为此将一切都置于危险之中并不是明智、成熟、聪明之举。

所以，我很抱歉，我们不能达成一致。

你永远的，
托尼
2006 年 9 月 6 日，星期三

---

① prospect [ˈprɔspekt] n. 景色，前景，前途

51. Tony Blair's Letter to MFAW

英国"反战军属"(Military Families Against the War)由数十名妇女组成,她们的丈夫、儿子或女儿正在伊拉克服役。2006年5月,"反战军属"的成员们向政府请愿,要求布莱尔首相接见她们,希望英军能从伊拉克撤出。布莱尔给她们写下了以下的这封信,说明了英军在伊拉克所执行的任务。

22 May 2006

Dear Military Families,

  Thank you for your letter in which you request a meeting to discuss your views. I have, in the past, met families who have lost loved ones in Iraq and other military operations involving UK forces. I know that Adam Ingram, has met a number of your group in recent months on an individual basis and that John Reid has met the families of the six Royal Military Policemen who were killed at al Majarr al Kabir. I can promise that the points raised in those meetings are being followed up actively.

  In your letter you accuse me of lying in order to take us into war with Iraq. I would like to make clear that this is simply not true. A number of inquiries, including the Hutton and Butler reports, found that no one in Government lied or fabricated① intelligence. I know many people continue to disagree with the Government's policies towards Iraq and ordering our forces to take action in Iraq was one of the most difficult decisions I have ever had to make, but I genuinely② believe it was the right decision.

  I do recognize the very real sacrifices being made by those involved in operations in Iraq and my deepest sympathies go out to all those who have

---

① fabricate [ˈfæbrikeit] v. 制作,构成,捏造,伪造
② genuinely [ˈdʒenjuinli] adv. 真诚地,诚实地

lost loved ones in Iraq. But we must stand alongside the Iraqi people and support them in their quest to establish democracy and in their fight against terrorism①.

I strongly believe that the Iraqi people do want democracy rather than the tyranny② they suffered for so long. The Iraqi Government has stated that they want us to stay in Iraq until they can deliver security themselves and we will not shrink from this commitment③.

I know our Armed Forces and their families have made sacrifices and I am immensely④ proud of them. I hope you will believe me when I say that I am sure that all those who have been killed in Iraq died defending their country and making the world safer for all of us. Once again, I offer my deepest sympathies to all those who have lost loved ones in Iraq.

Yours sincerely,
Tony Blair

托尼·布莱尔致"反战军属"

亲爱的军属们:

感谢你们的来信,在信中你们要求会见你们并讨论你们的看法。我曾经接见了一些在伊拉克战争及其他军事行动中失去亲人的英军家属。我知道亚当·英格拉姆已经以个人名义在近几个月接见了你们中的一部分,约翰·里德也接见了在马加尔卡比尔被杀的六位皇家宪兵的家属。我保证在那些会见中你们所提出的问题会被积极地对待。

在信里,你们指责我为了让大家参加伊拉克战争而撒谎,我想澄清这完全不是事实。许多调查,包括赫顿和巴特勒报告,都发现政府中的任何人都没有撒谎或谎报军情。我知道很多人继续反对政府对待伊拉克的政策,而命令我们的部队在伊拉克采取行动也是我曾经必须做的最难的决定之一,

---

① terrorism [ˈterəriz(ə)m] n. 恐怖主义
② tyranny [ˈtirəni] n. 暴政,苛政
③ commitment [kəˈmitmənt] n. 委托事项,许诺
④ immensely [iˈmensli] adv. 无限地,广大地

但是我真的相信那是正确的决定。

　　我确实认识到伊拉克行动中那些士兵所做的牺牲,我将最深的同情给予那些已经在伊拉克失去亲人的军属们。但是我们必须与伊拉克人并肩站在一起,并支持他们建立民主和打击恐怖主义的斗争中。

　　我坚信伊拉克人民渴望的是民主而非长久以来遭受的暴政。伊拉克政府已经声明他们想要我们留在伊拉克直到他们能处理安全问题为止,我们对此义不容辞。

　　我知道我们的武装部队以及他们的家庭所做出的牺牲,我为他们感到无比骄傲。我希望你们相信我,所有那些在伊拉克牺牲的士兵是为了保护他们的国家,使世界更加安全而献出自己宝贵生命的。再一次,我将我最深的同情献给那些在伊拉克失去亲人的家庭。

你们诚挚的
托尼·布莱尔
2006 年 5 月 22 日

52. MFAW's Letter to Tony Blair

对于布莱尔首相在信中所作的解释,"反战军属"的代表们持反对意见,她们坚持要得到首相的正式接见。在下面的这封信中,代表们指出赫顿和巴特勒对伊拉克战争的报告不真实,她们要求英国政府尽快从伊拉克撤军。

10 June 2006

Dear Prime Minister,

Thank you for your letter of 22 May 2006 in response to① our request that you meet with the Military Families campaign.

Contrary to what you suggest, there has never been a formal collective meeting between yourself and the bereaved② families wishing to attend.

As you are aware, members of the Military Families campaign have asked for such a meeting on numerous occasions. Recently more than 20 families whose loved ones died in Iraq came to Downing Street with this request. There are now more than 100 families, including a large number of families whose sons and husbands are serving in Iraq and Afghanistan, who would appreciate such a meeting.

You refer to the Hutton and Butler reports and say that these inquiries "found that no one in Government lied or fabricated intelligence".

The Hutton report has become a byword③ for whitewash and cover-up. Lord Hutton defined his terms of reference extremely narrowly.

---

① in response to 响应,适应
② bereaved [bi'ri:vd] adj. 失去亲人的
③ byword ['baiwə:d] n. 格言,谚语,笑柄

But even the Hutton inquiry revealed that the dossier① claim that Iraq "can deliver chemical and biological agents using an extensive range of artillery shells, free-fall bombs, sprayers and ballistic missiles... the Iraq military are able to deploy these weapons within 45 minutes of a decision to do so" was false and known to be false by you at the time.

The invasion of Iraq was one of option, not necessity. The trust of our armed forces was betrayed. Iraq never possessed weapons of mass destruction and had no links with Al Qaeda or any involvement with 9/11.

You say "all those who died in Iraq died defending their country". This is not the case—we are immensely proud of our sons and husbands. But they died serving their country.

Iraq posed no military threat to this country whatsoever. We believe that you abused the trust of our armed forces by sending them to war under a false premise.②

We are seeking a full independent inquiry into the decisions that were made that took us to war. Neither the Hutton nor the Butler inquiry undertook this task.

Such an inquiry would also examine the legal basis for the war and would investigate③ why you did not show the Cabinet the Attorney General's full legal advice. What made the Attorney General change his position about the legality④ of the war between the 7th and the 17th of March?

You now say we have a duty to "establish democracy in Iraq", but the Iraqi people want us to leave their country. This war has been responsible for the deaths of 113 members of the British armed forces

---

① dossier ['dɔsiei] n. [法] 档案,卷宗
② premise ['premis] n. [逻][法]前提
③ investigate [in'vestigeit] v. 调查,研究
④ legality [li(:)'gæliti] n. 合法

and for the deaths of many tens of thousands of Iraqis.

We believe that our troops should be brought home.

We ask you to meet with us at the earliest opportunity.

Rose Gentle

Reg Keys

on behalf of MFAW

"反战军属"致托尼·布莱尔

敬爱的首相：

谢谢您2006年5月22日对我们要求您会见军人家属的信件的答复。

与您的说法相反,从来就没有一个在您自己与想出席会晤的死者家属之间的正式的集体会晤。

如您所知,军属已经无数次要求举行这样的会面。最近20多家在伊拉克丧生的死者亲人,带着这个要求来到唐宁街首相官邸。目前有100多个家庭,其中很多人的儿子和丈夫都在伊拉克和阿富汗服役,都非常希望举行这样的一次会面。

您提到赫顿和巴特勒报告,说这些调查都发现政府中的任何人都没有人撒谎或谎报军情。

赫顿报告已经成为粉饰和掩盖的代名词,赫顿勋爵所提内容范围极窄。

即使是赫顿报告也证明档案显示"伊拉克可以提供生化制剂制成的远程炮弹、自由落体炸弹、喷雾器和弹道导弹……伊拉克军队能够在做出决定的45分钟内部署这些武器"是错误的,那个时候你也知道这是错误的。

入侵伊拉克只是一种选择,而不是必需,我们武装部队的信任被背叛了。伊拉克从未拥有大规模杀伤性武器,并没有同基地组织参与任何与9·11相关活动的迹象。

你说"所有那些在伊拉克牺牲的士兵都是为了保护他们的国家",事实并非如此——我们为我们的儿子和丈夫感到非常自豪,但他们是为国服务而牺牲的。

伊拉克并没有对我们国家构成任何军事威胁。我们认为您是

在一个错误的假设下滥用我们军队的信任把他们送进战争。

我们正在寻找一个独立的部门来调查这个把我们带进战争的决定。无论是赫顿还是巴特勒，都不能胜任这项任务。

这项调查还将审查发动战争的法律依据，并会调查您为什么没有出示内阁律政司的全部法律意见。从3月7日到17日，是什么使律政司改变了它所持的战争合法与否的立场？

您现在说，我们有责任"在伊拉克建立民主"，但是伊拉克人民希望我们离开他们的国家。这场战争必须对已经死亡的113名英国士兵和成千上万的伊拉克人负责。

我们认为我们的军队应该回家了。

我们请您在最短的时间内与我们会晤。

反战军属代表：
罗丝·简特尔
瑞格·克伊
2006年6月10日

53. George W. Bush's Letter to Ariel Sharon

"脱离接触计划"是以色列总理沙龙"单边行动计划"的正式名称,又被反对派称为"撤退计划",其核心内容是以色列定于 2005 年 8 月 15 ~ 17 日开始分阶段撤出加沙全部 21 个定居点和西岸 4 个定居点,将其移交给巴勒斯坦当局控制,从而减少巴以之间的暴力"接触",避免以色列平民和军人的伤亡。在下面的信中,美国总统布什与以色列总理沙龙就"脱离接触计划"和"中东路线图计划"展开讨论。

His Excellency
Ariel Sharon
Prime Minister of Israel
Dear Mr. Prime Minister,

  Thank you for your letter setting out your disengagement① plan.

  The United States remains hopeful and determined to find a way forward toward a resolution of the Israeli-Palestinian dispute②. I remain committed to my June 24, 2002 vision of two states living side by side in peace and security as the key to peace, and to the road map as the route to get there.

  We welcome the disengagement plan you have prepared, under which Israel would withdraw certain military installations③ and all settlements from Gaza, and withdraw certain military installations and settlements in the West Bank.

  These steps described in the plan will mark real progress toward realizing my June 24, 2002 vision, and make a real contribution toward peace. We also understand that, in this context, Israel believes it is

---

  ①   disengagement ['dɪsɪn'geɪdʒmənt] n. 脱离
  ②   dispute [dɪs'pjuːt] v. 争论,辩论
  ③   installation [ˌɪnstə'leɪʃən] n. 安装,设施

important to bring new opportunities to the Negev① and the Galilee②. We are hopeful that steps pursuant to③ this plan, consistent with my vision, will remind all states and parties of their own obligations under the road map.

The United States appreciates the risks such an undertaking represents. I therefore want to reassure you on several points.

First, the United States remains committed to my vision and to its implementation④ as described in the road map. The United States will do its utmost to prevent any attempt by anyone to impose any other plan. Under the road map, Palestinians must undertake an immediate cessation⑤ of armed activity and all acts of violence against Israelis anywhere, and all official Palestinian institutions must end incitement⑥ against Israel.

The Palestinian leadership must act decisively against terror, including sustained, targeted, and effective operations to stop terrorism and dismantle⑦ terrorist capabilities and infrastructure⑧. Palestinians must undertake a comprehensive and fundamental political reform that includes a strong parliamentary democracy and an empowered prime minister.

Second, there will be no security for Israelis or Palestinians until they and all states, in the region and beyond, join together to fight terrorism and dismantle terrorist organizations.

---

① Negev [ˈnegev] 内盖夫，以色列南部的山丘沙漠地区。1948 年巴勒斯坦被分割后划给以色列，它有大量的矿产资源。
② Galilee [ˈgæləˌli] 加利利，以色列北部地区。在巴勒斯坦最北部和以色列的古王国，加利利是基督教徒的中心。
③ pursuant to 按照，与……一致
④ implementation [ˌimplimenˈteiʃən] n. 执行
⑤ cessation [səˈseiʃən] n. 停止
⑥ incitement [inˈsaitmənt] n. 刺激，激励物
⑦ dismantle [disˈmæntl] v. 拆除
⑧ infrastructure [ˈinfrəˌstrʌktʃə] n. 下部构造，基础设施

The United States reiterates① its steadfast commitment to Israel's security, including secure, defensible borders, and to preserve and strengthen Israel's capability to deter② and defend itself, by itself, against any threat or possible combination of threats.

Third, Israel will retain its right to defend itself against terrorism, including to take actions③ against terrorist organizations. The United States will lead efforts, working together with Jordan, Egypt, and others in the international community, to build the capacity and will of Palestinian institutions to fight terrorism, dismantle terrorist organizations, and prevent the areas from which Israel has withdrawn④ from posing a threat that would have to be addressed by any other means.

The United States understands that after Israel withdraws from Gaza and/or parts of the West Bank, and pending agreements on other arrangements, existing arrangements regarding control of airspace, territorial waters, and land passages of the West Bank and Gaza will continue.

The United States is strongly committed to Israel's security and well-being as a Jewish state. It seems clear that an agreed, just, fair, and realistic framework for a solution to the Palestinian refugee issue as part of any final status agreement will need to be found through the establishment of a Palestinian state, and the settling of Palestinian refugees there, rather than in Israel.

As part of a final peace settlement, Israel must have secure and recognized borders, which should emerge from negotiations between

① reiterate [riːˈitəreit] v. 反复地说,重申
② deter [diˈtəː] v. 阻止
③ take actions 采取行动,提出诉讼
④ withdraw [wiðˈdrɔː] v. 撤退

the parties in accordance with UNSC Resolutions 242 and 338. In light of new realities on the ground, including already existing major Israeli populations centers, it is unrealistic to expect that the outcome of final status negotiations will be a full and complete return to the armistice① lines of 1949, and all previous② efforts to negotiate a two-state solution have reached the same conclusion.

It is realistic to expect that any final status agreement will only be achieved on the basis of mutually③ agreed changes that reflect these realities. I know that, as you state in your letter, you are aware that certain responsibilities face the State of Israel. Among these, your government has stated that the barrier being erected by Israel should be a security rather than political barrier, should be temporary rather than permanent, and therefore not prejudice any final status issues including final borders, and its route should take into account④, consistent with security needs, its impact on Palestinians not engaged in terrorist activities.

As you know, the United States supports the establishment of a Palestinian state that is viable⑤, contiguous⑥, sovereign, and independent, so that the Palestinian people can build their own future in accordance with my vision set forth in June 2002 and with the path set forth in the road map.

The United States will join with others in the international community to foster the development of democratic political institutions and new leadership committed to

① armistice [ˈɑːmistis] n. 停战,休战
② previous [ˈpriːvjəs] adj. 在前的,早先的
③ mutually [ˈmjuːtʃuəli] adv. 互相地,互助
④ take into account 重视,考虑
⑤ viable [ˈvaiəbl] adj. 能养活的,能生育的,可行的
⑥ contiguous [kənˈtiɡjuəs] adj. 邻近的,接近的

those institutions, the reconstruction of civic institutions, the growth of a free and prosperous economy, and the building of capable security institutions dedicated to maintaining law and order and dismantling terrorist organizations.

A peace settlement negotiated between Israelis and Palestinians would be a great boon not only to those peoples but to the peoples of the entire region.

Accordingly, the United States believes that all states in the region have special responsibilities: to support the building of the institutions of a Palestinian state; to fight terrorism, and cut off all forms of assistance to individuals and groups engaged in terrorism; and to begin now to move toward more normal relations with the State of Israel.

These actions would be true contributions to building peace in the region. Mr. Prime Minister, you have described a bold① and historic initiative that can make an important contribution to peace. I commend your efforts and your courageous decision which I support. As a close friend and ally, the United States intends to work closely with you to help make it a success.

Sincerely,
George W. Bush

乔治·W. 布什致阿里尔·沙龙

以色列总理
阿里尔·沙龙
阁下
亲爱的总理先生：

感谢您来信阐述了您的脱离接触计划。

美国仍满怀希望并决心寻求一条解决巴以争端的途径。我仍然坚持我2002年6月24日的设想，只有两国和平并安全地共存才是实现和平的关键，我致力于达到这个目的的路线图方案。

---

① bold [bəuld] adj. 大胆的

我们欢迎您提出的脱离接触计划,以色列将从加沙地带撤出部分军事设施和所有定居点,以及从西岸撤回部分军事设施和部分定居点。

计划中的这些步骤标志着实现我在 2002 年 6 月 24 日提出的设想的真正进展,为走向和平做出真正的贡献。我们也理解,在这一背景下,以色列认为这个计划为内盖夫和加利利问题的解决提供了新的机遇,这一点很重要,我们希望这个与我国方案一致的步骤,将提醒所有国家和当事方在这个路线图中的义务。

美国赞赏这种颇具风险的承诺。因此,我想对你做出几点保证。

首先,美国仍然保证执行我国提出的路线图计划,美国将尽全力防止任何人实施其他任何计划的企图。根据路线图,巴勒斯坦人必须承诺,立即停止武装活动和在任何地方所有针对以色列人的暴力行为,所有巴勒斯坦官方机构必须停止针对以色列的煽动行为。

巴勒斯坦领导人必须采取果断行动打击恐怖主义,包括持续的、有针对性和有效的行动来阻止恐怖主义和摧毁恐怖分子的能力和基础设施。巴勒斯坦必须进行全面的、根本的政治改革,要有一个强大的议会民主制度和经授权的总理。

第二,不管是以色列人还是巴勒斯坦人,除非他们和周边国家共同打击恐怖主义,解散恐怖组织,否则,他们将没有安全可言。

美国重申其对以色列安全的坚定承诺,包括安全、防卫边界,并维护和加强以色列的自身保护能力,抵抗任何威胁或可能产生的各种威胁。

第三,以色列将保留其自卫权利,以打击恐怖主义,包括对恐怖组织采取行动。美国将努力与约旦、埃及和其他国际社会一道发挥作用,建立一个有能力和意志的巴勒斯坦机构,以打击恐怖主义,解散恐怖组织,并防止以色列已撤出地区遭到各种威胁。

美国的理解是,在以色列撤出加沙和/或约旦河西岸部分地区,并就其他安排达成协议之前,约旦河西岸和加沙地区的领空、领海和陆地通道的实际控制权保持不变。

美国坚决致力于维护以色列作为一个犹太国家的安全和福祉。似乎很清楚，将需要通过建立一个共同认可的、公正、公平、现实的框架来解决巴勒斯坦难民问题，这个框架将是任何最终地位协议的一部分，这就需要建立一个巴勒斯坦国家，将难民安置在那里，而不是在以色列。

作为最终和平方案的一部分，以色列必须有安全和公认的边界，这应当出现在由当事者依照安理会 242 号和 338 号决议进行的协商之中。根据新的现实为依据，包括现有的以色列主要人口中心，期望最终地位谈判的结果为全面和彻底恢复到 1949 年的停火线那是不切实际的，以前所有的解决两国问题的谈判努力也都得出了相同的结论。

只有以共同认可的、反映现实情况的变更为基础，才能达成最终地位协议，这一期待切合实际。我知道，正如您在信中所述的，您认识到以色列所面临的某种责任，其中，贵国政府已表明以色列所设置的隔离带应是一个安全保障，而非政治障碍，应是暂时的，而非永久的，因此不会妨碍任何最终地位问题，包括最终边界，其路线应考虑进去，要与安全需要一致，还包括对不从事恐怖活动的巴勒斯坦人的影响。

如您所知，美国支持建立一个可行的、毗邻的、有主权的、独立的巴勒斯坦国，按照我在 2002 年 6 月提出与设定的路线图计划，巴勒斯坦人民能够建设自己的未来。

美国将与其他国际社会一起促进发展民主政治体制和效忠这些体制的新领导层，重建民间机构，发展自由繁荣的经济，建立有能力维护法律和秩序、打击恐怖组织的安全机构。

巴以谈判中的安全定居点不仅对于这两国人民，而且对于整个地区的人民都是一件大好事。

因此，美国认为，在该地区的所有国家有着特殊的责任：支持巴勒斯坦国的建立；打击恐怖主义，切断对从事恐怖活动的个人或团体的一切形式的援助；并从现在开始走向与以色列国的关系正常化。

这些活动将是对建立本地区和平的真正贡献。总理先生，您刚才所说的一个大胆的历史性举措是对和平的重要贡献，我非常赞赏您的努力和大胆的决定，这同样是我支持的。作为一名亲密朋友和盟友，美国有意与您密切合作，并使该计划成功。

真诚的

乔治·W. 布什

54. Ariel Sharon's Letter to George W. Bush

　　阿里尔·沙龙1928年出生于以色列特拉维夫沙龙山谷的一个犹太农民家庭,沙龙家原姓施恩内曼,后来才改以家庭所在地的沙龙山谷为姓氏。1966年,沙龙被任命为以色列国防军作训部队司令。1967年军衔升为少将。1981年,沙龙被贝京总理任命为国防部长。1999年9月2日当选为利库德集团新任领导人。在绝大多数渴望和平的以色列民众眼中,沙龙永远是一只好斗的"战鹰"。

Dear Mr. President,

　　The vision that you articulated in your 24 June 2002 address constitutes① one of the most significant contributions toward ensuring a bright future for the Middle East. Accordingly, the State of Israel has accepted the roadmap, as adopted by our government. For the first time, a practical and just formula② was presented for the achievement of peace, opening a genuine window of opportunity for progress toward a settlement between Israel and the Palestinians, involving two states living side-by-side③ in peace and security.

　　This formula sets forth the correct sequence and principles for the attainment of peace. Its full implementation represents the sole means to make genuine progress. As you have stated, a Palestinian state will never be created by terror, and Palestinians must engage in a sustained④ fight

---

① constitute ['kɔnstitjuːt] v. 制定(法律),建立(政府),组成,任命
② formula ['fɔːmjulə] n. 公式,规则,客套语
③ side-by-side 并肩的,并行的
④ sustained [səs'teind] adj. 持续不变的,相同的

against the terrorists and dismantle their infrastructure. Moreover, there must be serious efforts to institute true reform and real democracy and liberty including new leaders not compromised by terror. We are committed to this formula as the only avenue through which an agreement can be reached. We believe that this formula is the only viable one.

The Palestinian Authority under its current leadership has taken no action to meet its responsibilities under the roadmap. Terror has not ceased, reform of the Palestinian security services has not been undertaken, and real institutional reforms have not taken place. The State of Israel continues to pay the heavy cost of constant terror. Israel must preserve its capability to protect itself and deter its enemies, and we thus retain our right to defend ourselves against terrorism and to take actions against terrorist organizations.

Having reached the conclusion that, for the time being, there exists no Palestinian partner with whom to advance peacefully toward a settlement and since the current impasse① is unhelpful to the achievement of our shared goals, I have decided to initiate a process of gradual disengagement with the hope of reducing friction② between Israelis and Palestinians. The Disengagement Plan is designed to improve security for Israel and stabilize our political and economic situation. It will enable us to deploy③ our forces more effectively until such time that conditions in the Palestinian Authority allow for the full implementation④ of the roadmap to resume.

I attach, for your review, the main principles of the Disengagement Plan. This initiative, which we are not undertaking under the roadmap, represents an independent Israeli plan, yet is not inconsistent with the roadmap. According to this plan, the State of Israel intends to relocate

---

① impasse [æm'pɑːs] n. 僵局
② friction ['frikʃən] n. 摩擦, 摩擦力
③ deploy [di'plɔi] v. 部署
④ implementation [ˌimplimen'teiʃən] n. 执行

military installations and all Israeli villages and towns in the Gaza Strip, as well as other military installations and a small number of villages in Samaria①.

In this context, we also plan to accelerate② construction of the Security Fence, whose completion is essential in order to ensure the security of the citizens of Israel. The fence is a security rather than political barrier, temporary rather than permanent, and therefore will not prejudice any final status issues including final borders. The route of the Fence, as approved by our Government's decisions, will take into account, consistent with security needs, its impact on Palestinians not engaged in terrorist activities.

Upon my return from Washington, I expect to submit the Plan for the approval of the Cabinet and the Knesset, and I firmly believe that it will win such approval.

The Disengagement Plan will create a new and better reality for the State of Israel, enhance its security and economy, and strengthen the fortitude③ of its people. In this context, I believe it is important to bring new opportunities to the Negev and Galilee. Additionally, the Plan will entail a series of measures with the inherent④ potential to improve the lot of the Palestinian Authority, providing that it demonstrates the wisdom to take advantage of this opportunity. The execution of the Disengagement Plan holds the prospect of stimulating⑤ positive changes within the Palestinian

---

① Samaria [sə'mɛəriə] 撒玛利亚：巴勒斯坦中部一古城，位于现今约旦的西北部，该城作为以色列北部王国的首都建于公元前 9 世纪，又称撒玛里亚，于 721 年被二世征服，2 世纪时被希律一世大帝推毁并重建，据传说施洗者圣约翰埋葬于此。
② accelerate [æk'seləreit] v. 加速，促进
③ fortitude ['fɔːtitjuːd] n. 坚韧
④ inherent [in'hiərənt] adj. 固有的，内在的
⑤ stimulate ['stimjuleit] v. 刺激，激励

Authority that might create the necessary conditions for the resumption① of direct negotiations.

　　We view the achievement of a settlement between Israel and the Palestinians as our central focus and are committed to realizing this objective. Progress toward this goal must be anchored exclusively in the roadmap and we will oppose any other plan.

　　In this regard, we are fully aware of the responsibilities facing the State of Israel. These include limitations on the growth of settlements; removal of unauthorized outposts; and steps to increase, to the extent permitted by security needs, freedom of movement for Palestinians not engaged in terrorism. Under separate cover we are sending to you a full description of the steps the State of Israel is taking to meet all its responsibilities.

　　The government of Israel supports the United States' efforts to reform the Palestinian security services to meet their roadmap obligations to fight terror. Israel also supports the American's efforts, working with the International Community, to promote the reform process, build institutions and improve the economy of the Palestinian Authority and to enhance② the welfare of its people, in the hope that a new Palestinian leadership will prove able to fulfill③ its obligations under the roadmap.

　　I want to again express my appreciation for your courageous leadership in the war against global terror, your important initiative to revitalize④ the Middle East as a more fitting home for its people and, primarily, your personal friendship and profound⑤ support for the State of Israel.

Sincerely,
Ariel Sharon

① resumption [ri'zʌmpʃən] n. 取回,恢复,再开始
② enhance [in'hɑːns] v. 提高,增强
③ fulfill [ful'fil] v. 履行,实现,完成
④ revitalize ['riː'vaitəlaiz] v. 使新生,使复兴
⑤ profound [prə'faund] adj. 深刻的,意义深远的

阿里尔·沙龙致乔治·W.布什

亲爱的总统先生：

您在2002年6月24日提出的设想为确保中东有一个光明未来做出了最重大的贡献，因此，正如我国政府一样，以色列国接受并采纳路线图。这是第一个切实可行的公正的方案，它旨在实现和平，为解决以色列和巴勒斯坦人在和平与安全下共同生存问题打开了一扇真正的窗户。

这个方案为实现和平提出了正确的顺序和原则。全面落实是取得真正的进展的唯一方法。正如您所说的那样，巴勒斯坦国绝不会在恐怖主义中产生，巴勒斯坦人必须持续与恐怖分子作斗争，并摧毁他们的基础设施。此外，必须认真努力去开始真正的改革和真正的民主和自由，包括新领导人不对恐怖妥协。我们坚信这一方案是可以达成协议的唯一途径，我们相信这一方案是唯一切实可行的。

巴勒斯坦权力机构在现任领导下一直没有依据路线图采取行动，以履行其职责。恐怖行动没有停止，巴勒斯坦安全机构的改革尚未展开，而真正的机构改革并没有发生。以色列国继续为不断的恐怖威胁承受着沉重代价。以色列必须保持其实力，以保护自己和阻止敌人，因此，我们保留我们的权利来保卫自己免受恐怖主义的危害，并采取行动对付恐怖组织。

我们已得出结论，从一开始，就不存在与我们一起和平地走向解决方案的巴勒斯坦伙伴，因为目前的僵局无助于实现我们的共同目标，我已决定着手逐步地进行脱离接触，希望借此减少以色列人和巴勒斯坦人之间摩擦。脱离接触计划是为了改善以色列的安全及稳定我们的政治和经济形势，它将使我们更有效部署我们的力量，直到巴勒斯坦民族权力机构全面实施恢复路线图计划。

随信附上《脱离接触计划》的主要原则供您参考。这一举措我们没有在路线图计划中进行，它是一个独立的以色列的计划，但并不违背路线图。根据这一计划，以色列国打算迁移军事设施和在加沙地带的所有以色列村庄和城镇，以及其他军事设施和在撒马利亚的一些村庄。

在这一背景下，我们还计划加速建设安全墙，它的竣工对于以色列公民的安全是至关重要的。隔离墙是一个安全设施，而非政治障碍；是临时的，而非永久的，因此不会妨碍任何最终地位问题，包括最终边界。我国政府所批准的隔离墙路线符合安全需求，将考虑对不从事恐怖活动的巴勒斯坦人的影响。

从华盛顿返回后，我会将这一计划提交内阁和议会，我深信它会得到批准。

脱离接触计划将创造一个新的更为美好的现实，提高以色列的安全与经济，并增强人民的毅力。在这种情形下，我相信这为内盖夫和加利利带来新的机遇是至关重要的。此外，倘若巴勒斯坦权力机构能够审时度势的话，该计划将会为改善其自身产生一系列内在潜力的措施。脱离接触计划的实施可望在巴勒斯坦权力机构内部产生积极的变化，可能为恢复直接谈判创造必要的条件。

我们认为解决以色列和巴勒斯坦之间的问题是我们的重中之重，并致力于实现这一目标。迈向这个目标，必须专注着眼于路线图计划，我们将反对任何其他计划。

在这方面，我们充分认识到以色列面临的责任。这包括限制定居点的增长，撤除未经批准的前哨，并在安全需要许可的范围内，增加不从事恐怖活动的巴勒斯坦人的自由。我们会在另一封信中给你一个详尽的步骤说明，证明以色列国正在履行其全部责任。

以色列政府支持美国为改革巴勒斯坦安全机构，使他们执行对路线图的义务来打击恐怖主义而作出的努力。以色列同样支持美国与国际社会共同努力，促进改革进程，建立制度，改善巴勒斯坦权力机关的经济状况，提高巴勒斯坦人民的福利，以期新的巴勒斯坦领导阶层能够依照路线图计划履行它的义务。

我再次感谢您勇敢地领导着全球与恐怖行为作战，您为恢复中东作为一个更舒适的家园提出重要举措，最主要的是您个人的友谊和对以色列意义深远的支持。

真诚的
阿里尔·沙龙

55. Model Love Letters

I. This Is My Love

Dear,

As time goes on and we're apart, I think of how things should have been. I would have been more understanding and not so judgmental, more loving and not so hurtful. I would have told you I loved and cherished① you more often. There can never or will ever be another person who I admire like you or who has reached the depths of my heart as you have. I would have told you that I'm so very proud of how far you've come and the things you have accomplished. But how could I find the words or actions to explain to you just how much I love you. It would take a million lifetimes to even comprehend my feelings. I would have told you that you took my breath away the first time I saw you. I would have told you that I had fallen in love the first time you kissed me or you have stolen my heart the moment you uttered those magical  words. I would have told you that every time I looked into your eyes I saw my destiny. My one and only. My soul mate, my best friend, my lover, my husband, my inspiration, and the father of my children. I can still close my eyes and feel the softness of your lips against mine and your tender fingers as they caress② my body. I would have told you that my knees and entire body would shake every time you looked deep down into me with your eyes.

Life just isn't life without you. I wish that there were a way to make time stop and go back to a time when we were happy. We both know that

---

① cherish ['tʃeriʃ] v. 珍爱,怜爱,温柔地对待
② caress [kə'res] v. 抚爱

we need to change things about ourselves in order to make this relationship last. I hope that one day we can find a way to get past this, but until that day comes I want you to know that I will wait for you a lifetime because my love for you is never ending. Don't let our love fade away and our memories be scattered to the winds. I'll wait until you come back into my arms.

Erika

II. I'm Forever Yours

Dear Jesse,

　　There are no words to express how I feel about you. I constantly search for the words, and they all seem less than I truly feel. You are my life, my heart, and my soul. You are my one true love. I still remember the day we first met. I knew that you were the one I was meant to be with forever. As the years went by and we drifted apart, I still held onto the memory of you. I thought of you every day, and dreamed of you each night. Just when I thought you had forgotten me, you would call and make all my dreams seem real. The sound of your voice on the line was the sweetest sound I would ever find. Then one day you gave me a call, and told me I might have a chance to testify it all. My heart was beating hard within my chest. My hand was shaking and I could barely breathe. Then you came out to see me and I knew it was meant to be.

　　Those were the sweetest days of memories of the past. They went so quickly, I wanted them to last. The day you left, I wanted to die. You called me again, your voice on the line. I had to be near you, lying on your chest. I need to show you, that you were the best. So I made the decision to tell you how I feel. When you said you felt the same, I felt it was a dream. I packed up my stuff and altered my life. I never looked back. Now you will make me your wife. I seem to be on a

cloud, living in a dream, and a few days from now, it will really feel real. I wrote this letter for you to keep, and when you need a reminder of how I feel, just read it. I've said it before and I'll say it again, words cannot express how you make me feel. I make this promise to you my dear, to love you the way that you love me.

I now look to the future and forget the past, your life is mine and we will make it last. I love you more today than I did yesterday, and I'll love you more tomorrow than I do today. With all my heart I am forever yours.

Love always and forever,

Jennifer

Ⅲ. You Are Special

Dear Jimmy,

Life is so unpredictable. Changes always come along, in big or small ways. I don't know what happened that this sudden change has turned my world upside down. I don't know exactly what it is, it just hit me, but there is something really special about you.

It might be all the things I see on the surface, the things that everyone notices and admires about you, qualities, capabilities and a wonderful smile; these things set you apart from everyone else. But it may also be the big things: the person you really are that I hope to know more someday. And it might also be the little things: the way you walk and all your actions. I receive so much joy just being able to see a smile in your eyes. If I ever figure out the magic that makes you so special, I'd probably find out that it's a combination of all these things. You are a rare combination of so many special things. You are really amazing.

Inside of me there is a place where my sweetest dreams reside, where my highest hopes are kept alive, where my deepest feelings are felt and where my memories are safe and warm. I find that you're on my mind more often than any other thought. Sometimes I bring you there purposely just to make my day brighter. But more often, you surprise me and find your own ways into my thoughts. There are even times when I awaken, I realize that you've been a part of my dreams. Then during the day, when my imagination is free to run, it takes me into your arms and allows me to linger there knowing there's nothing I'd rather do. I know my thoughts are only reflecting the loving hopes of my heart because whenever they wander, they always take me to you.

　　Love Always,

Cathy

Ⅳ. Tender Love

Dear,

　　I'll always remember this day until my memory fades to black. It's as if I was awakened from my sleep. I felt like breathing again. I never thought that someone could make me feel this alive. I'd surely treasure those memories we've shared till I grow old. It is true—you'll never know true love till you get burned. You'll never realize what you got until you say goodbye.

　　I want to tell you many things. I want to share my feelings with you. I want to speak my heart out. I haven't mustered① enough courage to tell you how much I feel for you. What I want to say is I've loved you since day one. Since we said hellos, I know deep inside me, you'll be a part of me. I've loved everything about you. I've loved you clandestinely②; I kept it so hard I almost died inside.

　　It really pained me so much when I learned about the girl. I've loved you since day one. Those times when you were near, I waited untiringly. Yet I waited for nothing. Reality bites and it really broke my heart when I finally realized you never really loved me. I'm coping now but uncertain when I can really say I'm over you. I dread the day that you'd be getting married. I feel like I'm going to die.

---

① muster [ˈmʌstə] v. 召集,征召,鼓起
② clandestine [klænˈdestin] adj. 秘密的,暗中行事的

So I always ask Him to take away all these pains and let me move on with my life.

Love Always,

Marilyn

V. Forever

Dear Donnie,

Our love started with so much hope, so many dreams. It was a fairy tale that took us both by surprise. My Darling, my heart and soul belong to you. My destiny belongs in your hands.

Our memories are filled with so much joy and so much pain. In my heart I know the joy outweighs the pain. I want to embrace the joy and hold it close to my heart where it can live forever. I want to remember the pain as a lesson, a lesson of how much we almost lost. You and I have once more opened the door of conversation. I want to know the man you truly are. Donnie, we can never hide from each other again. This journey I ask you to walk with me will be joyous at times and rough. I don't offer you perfection. I offer you me, a woman who has weakness.

My love, I don't know how we are going to work through our problems, but I want you to know I am here for the long haul. I want to be with you for the rest of my life. I want you to be the first face I see when I awake and the last when I close my eyes to sleep. The last to hold my hand when I die.

I have never doubted my love for you, and have never doubted the love you have for me. How do you think I have survived the last 4 months? I had to leave you because knowing that love and not being able to express it or see it in your eyes was creating such sorrow in me. I felt like I was dying inside. It was the darkest hour of my life. Then you filled me with love, and brought me warmth and brightness.

I need you. I need to feel you in my arms. You don't know how hard

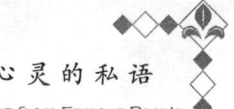

this is to admit to you. For I haven't admitted needing anyone. It really makes me feel vulnerable. Maybe with your help I won't have to feel this way any longer. I do need you, Donnie, as surely as I need to take my next breath.

I need us to hold hands and laugh together, love together, and also to cry together. My life is joined with yours my love. Not for the present but for the past and the future. Especially for the future. We are separated by so much distance but, Donnie, my love, you live in my heart. You are never far. All I have to do is think of you and you are here.

I wish I could offer you promises. I wish I could paint a future with no uncertainties. But I have none to offer. I have no idea what the future holds for us. I just know I want us to experience it together. I think it will be an adventure. We have shared so many, and they have never had to be earth shaking. They are the little ones that have climbed into our hearts and found a home. They are the kind that have created the sweetest memories.

Donnie, sometimes the thought of you takes my breath away with passion, sometimes I think of you and it's like the cleanest breath I have ever experienced, it calms and soothes me. Sometimes, it's like not breathing at all, it's like a long exhale and that's when I'm so sure of our love.

I am trying to be patient, and you know I'm probably the most impatient person in the world. I don't care how long it takes for us to work this out because I am so sure of the outcome. For me the outcome is a life of happiness.

My Darling, come dance with me for the rest of our lives.

Cynthia

情书范文

一、这就是我的爱

亲爱的：

随着岁月继续流逝，我们彼此分离，我想到了事情本该是什么样子。我

　　本该多一些理解,少一些判断;多一些爱护,少一些伤害;我本该告诉你我很珍爱你,不可能有、也决不会有我更倾慕的人了,没人会像你一样在我心中达到这样的深度;我本该告诉你,你一路奋斗而来,硕果累累,我非常为你感到骄傲。但是,我怎样找出词语和行动向你解释我有多爱你,理解我的感情要花去一百万辈子的时间。我本该告诉你,第一次我见到你,你就带走了我的呼吸;我本该告诉你,第一次你吻我时,我就爱上了你,当你说出那些有魔力的词语的那一刻,你偷走了我的心;我本该告诉你,每一次,我看着你的眼睛,就看见了我的命运。我的唯一、我的灵魂伴侣、我最好的朋友、我的情人、我的丈夫、我的灵感、我孩子的父亲。我闭上眼睛,就感到了你嘴唇的柔软和轻柔的手指抚慰我的身体。我本该告诉你,每一次你深深地凝望我,我的膝盖、我的整个身体都要颤抖。

　　没有你,生活就不是生活。我希望有什么方法让时间停止,回到我们快乐的时光。我们俩都知道,为了使这一关系保持下去,我们需要改变自身。我希望有一天我们能找出某个方法让这些过去,但是那一天到来之前,我想要你知道,我会用一辈子来等待你,因为我对你的爱决不会结束。不要让我们的爱凋谢,不要让我们的回忆随风飘散。我会等待着,直到你回到我的怀中,我爱你,从现在一直到死,永远永远。

艾丽卡

二、我永远属于你

亲爱的杰西:

　　没有语言能表达我对你的感受,我一直在搜寻恰当的词汇,但所有的词汇似乎都表达不了我对你的真实感受。你是我的生命、我的心、我的灵魂,是我唯一的真爱。我仍然记得我们第一天相遇,我知道你就是我终身相伴的人,年复一年地过去,我们也彼此分散,但我仍然将你保留在我的记忆中。我每天都想着你,每晚都梦着你。正当我以为你已经忘掉了我的时候,你给我来了电话,我所有的梦想似乎成了现实。你在电话上的声音是我能发现的最甜美的声音。然后,有一天,你打电话告诉我,我可能有机会证实一切。我的心在胸腔里嘣嘣直跳,手不停地颤动,几乎不能呼吸。然后你出来见我,我知道肯定是那么一回事。

　　那些是过去记忆中最甜蜜的日子。时光飞快流逝,我真希望它们能延续。你走的那一天,我想过死。你再次给我打电话,你的声音就在电话线上,我得靠近你,躺在你的胸上。我要让你明白你是我的最佳人选,所以我决定告诉你我的感觉。当你说你也有同样的感受,我感到好像是梦。我收拾了我的东西,改变了我的人生,决不回头。现在你要我成为你的妻子,我似乎飘上云端,生活在梦中。几天之后,这一切真的要成为现实。我给你写这封信,想要你保留,如果你想知道我的感受,你就阅读这封信。我前面说过,并还要再说一遍,语言无法表达我心中的感受。我向你保证,亲爱的,我爱你就像你爱我一样。

现在,我向往未来,忘掉过去,你的生命是我的,我们要它延续。我今天比昨天更爱你,明天又比今天更爱你,我全心全意地永远属于你。

永恒的爱

詹尼弗

三、你与众不同

亲爱的吉米:

生活如此难料,变化总是或大或小地出现。我不知道会发生什么,突如其来的变化将我的世界颠倒。我不知道究竟是什么打击了我,但是,你的的确确与众不同。

可能是我在表面上看到的一切,也是大家注意并且羡慕的一切:你的品行、能力和迷人的微笑,这些都使你与众不同。但也可能是些大事儿:你究竟是什么样的人,有朝一日,我想了解更多;也可能是些小事儿:你走路的方式和你的行为。能看到你眼中的笑容,我感到如此欢欣。如果我要找出是什么魔力使你如此与众不同,我可能会发现其实就是这一切的综合。你就是如此多的特殊品质的稀有综合,你真的很奇妙。

在我的内心有一个我最甜蜜的梦想居住的地方,那儿保存着我最高的希望,那儿能感受我最深的情感,在那儿,我的记忆安全而又温暖。我发现你比其他任何思绪更经常地占据我的心头。有时,我故意将你带到那个地方,使得我的白天更加明亮。但更多的时候,你让我惊奇,你总是走进我的想象。甚至有时候,我从梦中惊醒,发现你已成了梦的一部分。在白天,我的想象自由奔放,它将我带进你的怀抱,让我在那里停留,我知道我已别无他求。我的想象只反映了我心中爱的希望,因为无论什么时候它们漫游,它们总是将我带到你身旁。

永远的爱

凯西

四、温柔的爱

亲爱的：

我会永远记住这一天直到记忆褪成黑色,好像是我从睡梦中醒来,又感到了呼吸。我从没想到有人会使我感到如此充满活力。我肯定会珍惜我们共同拥有的这些记忆,直到我慢慢变老。真的,你只有到了被激情燃烧的时候才会感觉到真爱,你只有到了说再见的时候才会意识到你的拥有。

我想告诉你许多事情,我想同你分享我的感情,我想将心事向你坦诚。但我没有积聚足够的勇气向你表白我对你有多深的感情。我所想说的就是从第一天起我就爱上了你。自从我们说了声"你好",我就从内心深处知道你将成为我的一部分,我爱上了你的一切。我秘密地爱着你,我艰难地将它隐藏,以至于我几乎在内心里死亡。

当我得知有那个女孩,我真的感到非常忧伤。我第一天就爱上了你,那时你离我很近,我总是不知疲倦地等你。然而,我什么都没有等到,现实咬着我的心,使我心碎,我终于明白你从没有真正地爱过我。我现在正在进行激烈的斗争,却不知何时才能结束。你结婚的那一天会让我感到恐惧,我感到我要死去。所以我一直请求上帝将这些痛苦带走,让我继续自己的生活。

永远爱你!

玛丽琳

五、永　　远

亲爱的唐尼：

我们的爱始于如此多的希望和梦想,就像童话一样,让我们俩惊奇不已。亲爱的,我的心和灵魂属于你,我的命运就在你的手中。

我们的记忆里充满了欢欣和痛苦。在我的心中,我知道欢欣超过了痛苦。我想拥抱欢欣,将它紧紧地藏在心中,它在那儿可以永远生存。我想将痛苦记成教训,看看我们失去了多少。你和我曾经敞开对话的大门,我想知道你究竟是怎样的人。唐尼,我们决不能再躲躲藏藏了。我请求你跟我一起走的路程有时会充满欢乐,有时会充满艰辛。我不能给你提供完美,我只能给你提供我自己——一个有弱点的女人。

我的爱,我不知道怎样处理我们的问题,但是我要你知道我准备长期努力下去。我希望我的余生能和你在一起,我希望你是我醒来后看到的第一张面孔,是我睡着前看到的最后一张面孔,也是我死的时候最后一个和我握手的人。

我曾不怀疑我对你的爱,也不怀疑你对我的爱。你怎么也想象不到我过去四个月是如何度过的?我离开你是因为我无法表达我的爱,我也无法从你的眼中看见爱,这给我带来了很大的痛苦,我感到我的心要死了,那是我生命中最黑暗的日子。然后你用爱将我填满,给我带来温暖和光明。

我需要你,需要感觉你在我的怀中。你不知道向你承认这些该是多难哪!因为我从没承认我需要任何人,这真的让我感到很脆弱。也许有了你的帮助,我不再有这种感受。我需要你,唐尼,正像我需要呼吸一样千真万确。

我需要我们手拉着手,一起欢笑,一起爱,一起哭。我的生命与你交融,我的爱,不是为此刻,而是为过去和未来,尤其是为未来。我们已经被如此远的距离阻隔,但是,唐尼,我的爱,你一直在我的心中,从未远离。我所做的一切就是去想你,而你就在这里。

我希望我能给你保证,我希望我能描绘一个确确实实的未来,但是我什么都提供不了。我不知道我们的未来会是怎样,我只知道我想与你共同经历它。我想它会是冒险,我们已共同经历了许多事情,它们从不是什么地震,只是些小震动,爬进我们的心中,并在那儿安家。它们已成为最甜蜜的回忆。

唐尼,有时对你的强烈思念使我屏住呼吸;有时对你的思念就像是我呼吸过的最清新的空气,它让我平静,给我慰藉;有时它根本不像呼吸,就像长长地呼出一口气,那时我对我们的爱深信不疑。

我尽力忍耐,你知道我可能是世界上最有耐心的人,我不管我们会花多长时间将这些弄个明白,因为我对结果充满信心,对于我,结果就是幸福生活。

我亲爱的,让我们的余生一起共舞。

辛西娅

附录:英文书信的组成

英文书信一般由六部分组成。即:信头(Heading)、信内地址(Inside Address)、称呼(Salutation)、正文(Body of Letter)、结束语(Complimentary Close)、署名(Signature),有时在书信后面还有附言(Postscript)、附件(Enclosure),等等。

1. 信头(Heading)

信头是写信时最先写的部分,又称信端。信头一般写在信纸的右上角,包括寄信人的通信地址和写信日期。从信纸上首中间偏右处起,第一行先写寄信人的门牌号码,再写街道名称;第二行先写县市名称,再写省份名称,往右空两个字母宽的位置,再写上邮政编码。如果信是寄给国外的,寄信人还应该写第三行,这行写自己国家的名称,最后一行注上写信的日期。每行的后面可用标点符号,也可以不用。如用,前面几行的末尾都用逗号,写信日期的后面则用句号。

时间的写法对英国人和美国人而言是不同的。英国人习惯按日、月、年的顺序写,而美国人习惯按月、日、年的顺序写。例如:

英式:1st October,2007

美式:October 1,2007

在使用前一种形式时,月和年之间的逗号可用可不用,但是在后一种形式中,必须使用逗号。

信头有齐头和缩行两种格式,左边各行开头字母垂直排齐的叫齐头式;从第二行起,每行开头都比上行向右缩进两三个字母的叫缩行式。目前齐头式比较常用,因其在打字机或电脑上更便于操作,工作效率可以得到提高。

齐头式

　　1575 Oak Avenue Apt. 75
　　Evanston Illinois 60201
　　U. S. A.
　　Oct. 7,2007
　　美国伊利诺斯州埃文斯顿
　　奥克大街1575号75号公寓
　　2007年10月7日

缩行式
  Foreign Language Department,
   East China Normal University,
    Shanghai 200062,
     P. R. China,
      Nov. 8,2007.
中华人民共和国
  上海华东师范大学外语系
  2007 年 11 月 8 日

2. 信内地址(Inside Address)

信内地址要写出收信人的姓名和地址。一般给比较生疏的亲友的信和公事信件要写出信内地址,而熟悉朋友可以省去这一步骤。信内地址写在日期下一两行的左上角,第一行写收信人的称呼姓名,然后写出地址。地址也是从小到大写出,分缩进式和齐头式两种。例如:

Dr. David Fuller
Graduate Studies
Northern State University
1200 South Jay Street
Aberdeen,SD57401 – 7198
U. S. A.
美国南达科他州阿伯丁
南杰伊街 1200 号
北方州立大学研究生部
大卫·富勒博士

3. 称呼(Salutation)

称呼是对收信人的称谓。在信内地址下一两行处顶格写起,自成一行。末尾用逗号或冒号。

  (1)当给一位熟悉的人写信时可以用 Dear 或是 My Dear。在英国,My Dear 比 Dear 亲切,而在美国,Dear 比 My Dear 亲切。

  (2)当给一位你不知婚否的女性写信时,可以用 Ms…,这是指"……女士"。

  (3)在给不熟悉的人写信时,可以用 Dear Sir,Dear Madam,Dear Sirs,Gentleman 等等。

4. 正文(Body of Letter)

正文是一封信的主体部分。通常在称呼的下一行写出。正文也可采用齐头式或缩进式的方法。齐头式是指每段开头一行和后面行并齐。缩进式是指每段的第一行向右缩进几个字母。信笺讲究简洁、效率。开头几句简单地寒暄后就步入正题,在结尾处要有祝愿和敬语。

常用的开头语有:

①I have received your letter of July 1st. 7月1日来信已经收悉。

②I have the pleasure to tell you that …很高兴告诉你……

③I am very much delighted to receive your letter. 非常高兴收到你的来信。

④It is my honor to inform you that …很荣幸告诉你……

常用的结束套话有:

①I am looking forward to hearing from you. 盼早日回信。

②Best regards. 祝好。

③Thank you for your help. 感谢你的帮助!

④My best wishes for your success. 祝你成功。

⑤Wishing you a happy holiday. 祝假日愉快!

⑥Hoping to hear from you soon. 希望能尽快收到你的回信。

5. 结束语(Complimentary Close)

结束语在正文之后隔一两行的偏右方开始写出。开头字母用大写,以后的字母用小写,最后一个词后面用逗号。

常用的结束语有:

①一般非正式的关系:

Yours sincerely,

Yours truly,

Yours faithfully,

Most sincerely,

Faithfully yours,

②亲密的关系:

Love,

Yours love,

Yours Affectionately,

With love,

Lovingly yours,

Yours ever,

③上级和长者:

Yours respectfully,

Faithfully yours,

6. 署名(Signature)

在结束语的下方是署名,先用手写体,再用印刷体。如果收信人不认识写信人,可以在署名前用括号标出 Mr.,Miss 或 Ms。在名称下面可注上头衔。如:

Yours sincerely,

Lucy Blake（手写体）

Lucy Blake（Miss）（印刷体）

Sales Manager

7. 附言(Postscript),附件(Enclosure)

在信件正文写作时可能漏掉了某些事,或临时发生了某事需要补充时,可以在信下面左下方写上 P. S.（附言）。

如果随信有附件可在信的左下端注明。如:Enclosure:Resume（个人简历）。